GETTING THE TALK RIGHT

the chief executive press

GETTING THE TALK RIGHT

ROBERT GOLDBERG

whittle direct books

Photographs: Edwin L. Artzt by Louis Psihoyos/Matrix, page 9; William
J. Alley by Marianne Barcellona, page 21; Richard J. Stegemeier,
AP/Wide World Photos, page 23; Franklin D. Roosevelt, AP/Wide
World Photos, page 27; Ronald Reagan, AP/Wide World Photos, page
27; Bill Clinton, AP/Wide World Photos, page 27; Joseph
V. Vittoria by Jonathan Levine, page 29; Richard A. Clarke by Doug
Menuez/Reportáge, page 37; Robert J. Nugent, AP/Wide World
Photos, page 51; John R. Hall, courtesy of Ashland Oil, page 56; Lee
Iaccoca, UPI/Bettmann, page 73; John A. Young by Philip
Saltonstall/Onyx, page 82; Roy E. Verley by Robert Holmgren, page 82.

The Chief Executive Press: Dorothy Foltz-Gray, Editor;
Ken Smith, Design Director; Evelyn Ellis, Art Director

Library of Congress Catalog Card Number: 93-060993
Goldberg, Robert
Getting the Talk Right:
The CEO and the Media
ISBN 1-879736-19-5
ISSN 1060-8923

the chief executive press

The Chief Executive Press presents original short books by distinguished authors on subjects of special importance to the topmost executives of the world's major businesses.

The series is edited and published by Whittle Books, a business unit of Whittle Communications L.P. Books appear several times a year, and the series reflects a broad spectrum of responsible opinions. In each book the opinions expressed are those of the author, not the publisher or the advertiser.

I welcome your comments on this ambitious endeavor.

William S. Rukeyser
Editor in Chief

For Colleen

CONTENTS

PROLOGUE

ineteen ninety-three began with a bang for business— if media coverage is any indication. During the first two weeks alone:

• *The Wall Street Journal* reported that Ford Motor Company had introduced the Bronco II despite evidence that it tended "not only to tip, but to roll over completely at relatively moderate speeds." The article cited 200 lawsuits involving injury or death to Bronco passengers.

• *The New York Times* stated that a corrosion problem leading Portland General Electric Company to retire its Trojan nuclear plant in Rainier, Oregon, "will affect more reactors as the years go by." The owners face a painful decision, said the *Times*: "Make expensive repairs, or retire their plants, or cut their power ratings."

• *Fortune* reported that Microsoft would likely succeed IBM as "the world's most valuable company in the computer game." Citing earnings up 264 percent from January 1991, the article noted that Microsoft founder and CEO William H. Gates was "grinning broadly."

• *World News Tonight* of ABC announced that factory problems at Parke-Davis Pharmaceuticals in Morris Plains, New

Jersey, had reduced the U.S. supply of the vital heart drug nitro-glycerin. During the broadcast, an earnest-looking cardiologist stared into the camera and said, "It makes me very angry that the manufacturer didn't have the courtesy and responsibility to advise us."

• *Business Week* named Bernard Marcus, CEO of Home Depot, one of 1992's top managers. Said the report, "There's no slowing down Home Depot."

• *Variety* leaked a memo about a job freeze at ABC, noting, "It's going to be a cold, cold winter" for the company's employees.

Day after day, year after year, CEOs are surprised and sometimes angered by articles and broadcasts about their companies. As they look at the reports they may well ask, Why do some companies consistently get favorable coverage while others rarely get the benefit of the doubt? Why are some always in the limelight, others not? Most important, what can *I* do to help shape my company's reputation? Since the company will be talked about in the marketplace and in the wider world, how do we get the talk right?

Few CEOs fully understand the link between company stature and the company's relationship with the media. Yet most chief executives are good communicators. That's part of how they got to the top. Communication is a significant part of their job, and over the years they've had practice. So why aren't they getting the coverage they want?

Today almost every Fortune 500 executive has had some training in dealing with the media. Few, regardless of the size of their corporations, have escaped the media-training mills—the classrooms, flip charts, and video cameras. The current crop of chief executives is better versed in dealing with the press than any other in history. They've learned the tricks: Keep your eyes steady when looking into the TV camera. Don't wear a white shirt, which will glare under studio lights, or a finely striped suit, which will shimmer onscreen. Know the difference between "not for attribution" and "off the record." If you have bad news, return calls after the newspaper and TV deadlines; if the news is good, call back before. And, of course, master the sound bite.

What's been taught is a handful of gimmicks. They may be

useful, but after you've learned to wear a blue suit and red tie, after you've learned how to duck the difficult questions, then what? You can coast only so far on sound bites.

This book is about the next step—not just how to handle the tough interview, but how to think strategically about all your interactions with the press. It offers neither snappy tricks nor magic answers. (There are none, even if consultants argue otherwise.) What it does offer is a different way of thinking.

In my years as a writer, reporter, and media critic, I've been astounded by how sophisticated corporate America is in its dealings with the press—and yet how benighted. Businesses have spent a lot of time, effort, and money trying to understand these interactions. But with all the energy focused on process, the content questions have been misplaced: What's your long-term agenda for working with the media? What are you trying to say?

So here's what I propose: It's time business approached the media proactively, not reactively. That means taking charge of what you have to say, no longer allowing someone else's questions and agenda to define your message. It's time to concentrate on communicating for a reason—a business reason. With this approach the media and the accompanying exposure are no longer necessary evils but opportunities to aggressively further your business goals. To do that, you've got to understand how the press works. And you've got to build a long-term relationship with the media, to educate reporters about how you work, and to recognize the opportunities as they arise.

Above all, corporate leaders need to create a media plan that dovetails with their company's strategic plan. How do you create such a plan, and what should its goals be? Once you've nailed down a strategy, how do you put it into practice? Those are the questions we'll address in the following chapters. And along the way we'll also look at an old concept in a new guise—the concept of story.

First flight of the spectacular new Citation X business jet is just days away. So enthusiasm around Cessna is even higher than usual because we know the Citation X will shape corporate air transportation well into the next century.

If you fly long distances, speed and nonstop range are especially important. The new Citation X flies at .9 Mach, faster than any commercial jet except the Concorde. And its range exceeds 3700 miles.

Equally impressive is the Citation X's remarkably low cost of operation. In today's business environment, having the right combination of performance and economy is especially important.

The Citation X is exactly the right size, too. Seating eight in stand-up, walk-around comfort, it is half the cost of larger, less efficient corporate aircraft.

Initial deliveries of this truly phenomenal new aircraft are two years away, with production through 1996 already committed.

We look forward to telling you more about the Citation X as it takes to the air and makes aviation history.

Sincerely yours,

Russell W. Meyer, Jr.
Chairman and Chief Executive Officer
Cessna Aircraft Company

Cessna Aircraft Company · One Cessna Boulevard · Wichita, Kansas 67215 · 316/941-7400

Cessna
A Textron Company

Chapter One

WELCOME TO THE FRONT LINES

S ometime in the next few weeks or months or years, you and your company are going to get hammered in the press. That's just a cost of doing business. Maybe the information will be inaccurate, which is infuriating. Maybe it will be correct, which is worse.

Only you can gauge the impact of unfavorable coverage. But over the years all CEOs have seen TV and newspaper pieces that portray fellow CEOs as inept, reveal sensitive information, or tell only one side of the story. Such news can affect the price of stocks, bring regulators calling, and shake up entire management structures. It can even cost a CEO his job. No wonder company heads are leery of the press.

James F. Smith Jr., chairman of First American Corporation, a bank-holding company based in Nashville, believes "most CEOs feel an adversarial relationship with the press. They sense the news media have a more liberal perspective than CEOs do—and an initial bias against business." William J. Alley, CEO of American Brands, the corporate umbrella for products as diverse as Jim Beam whiskey, Pall Mall cigarettes, and Master locks, shares Smith's conclusions. "A lot of CEOs do become jaded and suspicious of dealings with the press," said Alley. "They think the press is looking for the warts, the sensational stuff. Whatever happened to objective reporting?" One Fortune 500 executive raised the question that eventually flits through every CEO's mind: "Why the hell should I even talk to the press?"

As a CEO, you are news. The press will write and talk about you whether you speak to reporters or not. The days of quietly going about your business disappeared with earth shoes and pet rocks.

In the 1960s and early '70s, most newspapers printed little about business other than a couple of stock tables and wire service reports buried at the back of the sports section. "For the typical metropolitan paper, business coverage was an afterthought," noted Paul E. Steiger, managing editor of *The Wall Street Journal*. "Business reporting was the burial ground for the least successful members of the staff."

Over the past two decades, financial journalism has changed dramatically. Some trace the turning point to the oil shocks of the '70s and the ensuing inflation and unemployment. Others say it took the go-go '80s, with the high rollers and leveraged buyouts, to transform business into news. Either way, financial reporting has become a nightly feature on national broadcasts, and as of 1993 almost all of the more than 1,000 U.S. metropolitan daily newspapers publish business sections. Financial reporting has escaped from the business ghettos to the front pages.

Business has become what journalists call sexy. The public, as well as the press, considers what you do important, even interesting. The downside is that now everyone wants to watch. Business leaders have to learn to operate under the glare. And as financial coverage gets broader and more sophisticated, the scrutiny will intensify.

That's only fair. The nation needs to understand the actions of business. The investors in publicly held companies have a right to know what those firms do with their money. Any company, public or private, large or small, makes decisions that affect its community—decisions about consumer safety and environmental responsibility, for example. And as the most significant player in rejuvenating the U.S. economy, business is sure to draw even more media attention in the coming years. The 1992 presidential election was essentially a referendum on the recession and the deficit. Some would argue that in the late '90s the battle for America's national security will be fought on economic terrain.

"These days it's not enough just to run a company and produce goods," said Richard J. Stegemeier, chairman and CEO of Unocal Corporation, the Los Angeles-based energy company. "You have to communicate what you're doing and how you're doing it. The old days of simply sending out the dividend checks— that's not sufficient anymore. You have to explain why you're not doing well, or why you are, and that what you're doing is legal and ethical. This is the communications generation. People demand to know what's going on."

Sooner or later circumstances will push almost every CEO in front of the cameras whether he likes it or not. The smart CEO will make a virtue of it, turning the spotlight into an opportunity—especially if he understands the relationship of media to business. Chief executives need to concentrate on this interaction, making a partnership with the press as much a part of their basic business strategy as keeping the ledger in the black. The motivation for doing so is not defensive but affirmative. At Quaker Oats, executives like to say that if they had to choose between holding on to their factories or their good name, they'd choose their good name every time. A solid reputation has a halo effect. And reputations are born in the press.

When listing their constituencies—suppliers, customers, bankers, employees—many CEOs include the media. This is fundamentally incorrect. In business a constituency is those directly involved in or served by a company. By that definition the press is not in itself a constituency but the principal pipeline to your constituencies, internal and external. The press can be a tool, a major tool in achieving crucial company objectives. Only the careless would discard such a tool.

Chapter Two

THE FOUR MEDIA APPROACHES

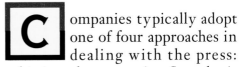ompanies typically adopt one of four approaches in dealing with the press: antimedia, media-neutral, sophisticated, or proactive. Some businesses take one of these paths; others tend to shift back and forth.

Antimedia. The antimedia approach is characteristic of old-style corporate thinking: "Maybe if we just ignore the press, it'll go away and let us get on with our jobs." The objective of this bunker mentality is to keep the press outside by enforcing a code of secrecy inside. Termed the mushroom strategy—keep 'em in the dark and spread the fertilizer around—this approach is fairly Neanderthal, and yet some successful companies practice it. "We don't see any reason to talk to the press," said one senior officer of Procter & Gamble. "We don't get anything out of it, and we only give away things we shouldn't."

The problem with this approach is that it won't keep the press from writing unfavorably about your company. Take the case of Alecia Swasy, the *Wall Street Journal* reporter who covered Procter & Gamble from 1988 to late 1991. In mid-1991 she wrote two stories describing the departure of executive vice-president B. Jurgen Hintz well before the company wanted that information made public. Chairman and CEO Edwin L. Artzt responded angrily and immediately. According to Swasy, Procter & Gamble "did an internal investigation to see who was calling my phone." When that turned up nothing, the company "called the police and got grand jury permission to go through the entire Cincinnati phone records to see if anybody in that area code was calling either my home or my office. P&G security went through 35 million toll calls. And the short list got invited down to the police station."

When the story broke, Artzt stonewalled. He defended P&G's actions, saying the company had every right under the Ohio trade-secrets law to act as it did. But as the story played out in the national press, exploding into headlines as a cautionary tale of Big Brother and corporate paranoia, Artzt was forced to recant. Swasy ended up with a big book deal. Artzt ended up with front-page articles across the country ridiculing him and his company.

Only a small percentage of companies consistently practice an antimedia strategy. A classic example of one that did is Mobil during Herbert Schmertz's years as vice-president of public affairs. From 1974 to 1988 Schmertz defined media relations as warfare. His strategy was to close ranks within the organization and keep the press on the defensive. In fact, he was so committed to bypassing the media that he bought advertising space in *The New York Times*, where he printed his own "stories."

Today most firms consider this posture counterproductive. Even companies that reporters once called arrogant and reclusive, like Boeing and American Home Products, a New York-based manufacturer of health-care goods, are rethinking their approach. Still, many corporations revert to the bunker mentality in times of stress.

Media-neutral. Most companies adopt this approach. Stuart F. Sucherman, president of Hilton-Sucherman Productions, a media-consulting firm whose clients include General Electric and GTE, feels that "the vast majority of companies live in a vacuum, in splendid isolation. They ignore the press. They view dealing with it like root canal surgery. And they certainly haven't thought about any strategy."

After all, most American businesses are small and have few

After Procter & Gamble CEO Ed Artzt defended the company's 1991 search of employee phone records, headlines painted a picture of corporate paranoia.

dealings with the media. Most have limited PR staffs or none at all. Media-neutral executives respond when the local paper calls, or they issue a press release from time to time.

William W. Sprague Jr., CEO of Savannah Foods and Industries, is a good example of an executive who espouses the media-neutral approach. "Media's not a big part of my job," he said. "Our company is not as visible as some others. Companies our size are liable to get media attention only if we screw up from an environmental point of view." Despite Sprague's modesty, Savannah Foods did $1.2 billion in sales in 1991 and was number 324 on the 1992 list of the Fortune 500. Still, Sprague estimates that press relations take up less than 5 percent of his time.

Sprague sees no necessity for a PR staff. "If something needs explaining," he said, "the top officer ought to do it. He knows the area; PR doesn't. If I hired a PR staff, what the hell is it going to talk about?"

Sprague's strategy—or rather, his *non*strategy—is legitimate but limited. There's little downside to it, but little upside either.

Sophisticated. Since the early '80s many companies have adopted a so-called sophisticated approach in their dealings with the press. They hire PR staffs or consultants like Burson-Marsteller or Hill & Knowlton, whose representatives make a lot of cold calls and send out a flurry of press releases.

The CEOs of such companies take media-training seminars and develop crisis-response plans. They learn the new buzzwords in press relations, like "openness" and "honesty," and throw them into their conversations with journalists to prove how open and honest they are. In the words of Timothy J. Doke, managing director of corporate communications for American Airlines, "We're forthright to the point of candor."

Sophisticated companies are not as numerous as media-neutral ones, but they are the industry leaders—the Fortune 500 and the Business Week 1,000. They have at their disposal specialized public-relations tools, such as Dean Rotbart's *TJFR Business News Reporter.*

Rotbart is one of many who profit from corporate America's fear of the press. His publication profiles the journalists he terms corporate assassins. The *Reporter* is "devoted to exposing the reporters and editors most likely to pummel the companies they cover and torpedo their stock prices," wrote Rotbart in a pamphlet promoting his newsletter. "As a result, subscribers to the newsletter are armed and ready when the journalistic wolves come clawing at their doors."

The 1,500 subscribers to the *Reporter* may be better prepared to anticipate a media attack. But the problem with this and other "sophisticated" approaches is that CEOs and their PR staffs may focus on the wrong issues—the minutiae of press relations and not the message. The important question is: What do you want to say?

Proactive. Companies with a proactive approach to media relations concentrate on communicating for clearly defined business reasons. They build long-term relationships with journalists, helping to ensure that the messages they consider crucial receive the desired coverage. Executives who use this stance have a consistent understanding of what they're trying to say and why. Consider the perennial positive press given Warren E. Buffett, chairman and CEO of Berkshire Hathaway, the huge conglomerate based in Omaha, Nebraska. Although Buffett may well deserve good press for his solid business record, he also works at it. He has long-standing relationships with key journalists. He stays in touch, updating them on his business ventures and providing them with fodder for other business stories as well. The press understands how Buffett works, and it shows in the coverage. His is the kind of foresight that companies like American Brands, Pacific Gas and Electric, and Levi Strauss are using to build their business reputations.

Many companies pay lip service to this kind of approach, especially those in the sophisticated group, but few have reached this plateau, and many keep slipping back into old patterns. Nevertheless, a proactive approach is without question the most effective in forming a long-term relationship with the media. And it starts with a media strategy.

IN REAL LIFE, THE HARE BEATS THE TORTOISE EVERY TIME.

For years, the turboprop industry has claimed that slow and steady wins the race. To say that a turboprop is somehow more sensible than a jet is a harebrained notion at best. At nearly 100 mph faster, the Citation II outperforms turboprops in every category, at operating costs guaranteed to be lower. And for virtually the same purchase price.

Today, the turboprop story is little more than a fairy tale. And the time has come, once and for all, to close the book on it.

THE SENSIBLE CITATIONS

Cessna
A Textron Company

Chapter Three

BUILDING A MEDIA STRATEGY

I f you've ever attended a media-training seminar, you've heard the cynical but apt credo for live TV and radio interviews: Don't answer the question. Say what you came to say. Instead of ceding control to the interviewer, steer the interview toward your ideas. "As soon as the word *media* comes up," said media consultant Jan D. Sempliner, "many executives picture an interrogation. But what's more important is the message *they* want to get across." A vice-president of Communispond, a New York-based media-consulting firm, Sempliner doesn't work with prefabricated questions and answers. "Instead we try to draw up a list of three to five statements executives want to see in print or on the air," she said.

That's the secret most media-training consultants charge thousands of dollars for: the interviewer gets to pick the questions, but you pick the answers. Of course, it takes practice to flow gracefully from his questions to your message, and the better the interviewer, the less you will get away with it. But it's a discussion, and you should have at least half the control.

Many CEOs have profited from this advice. They do more

than react to interview questions; they attempt to take charge. Surprisingly, few have transferred this maxim to the next step, from the single interview to all their press interactions. The same CEOs who take charge in one-on-one situations may allow reporters' phone calls to initiate and define their companies' overall media relations. Of course, some companies think they are evening the balance when they stage PR blitzes to launch a new product. Generally this barrage of predictable press releases is a waste of time for reporters and the company alike.

When most CEOs think about media relations, they think about shutting down the negative stories. Or they think about increasing name recognition of the company and its products. That makes perfect sense, but it's not a message, and it's not an effective plan. What most companies lack is a strong media agenda, a long-term strategy to get across a few key ideas about the company and its products or services. "Not many companies see how strong a well-defined media plan can be," said Sempliner.

Lack of focus is the norm among even the most sophisticated executives. When asked what message he would most like the media to print verbatim, Richard Detweiler, director of public relations for Pepsico, hemmed and hawed. "Pepsico is a company that everyone loves and wants to invest in," he said finally, "a company that's growth-oriented, with enlightened management and lots of opportunities rewarding to the investor."

That's a wonderful sentiment, but it's not a message. It contains nothing concrete for a viewer or reader to care about. And it does nothing to advance Pepsico's cause. All it says is, I work for a wonderful company that deserves lots of attention, and I want everyone to love my company.

Detweiler is not unique. In fact, few executives could do better. Media guru Gershon Kekst, whose public-relations firm Kekst and Company represents everyone from Xerox and Polaroid to Toys "R" Us and the Gap, tells the following story: "I was having lunch with the number-two man in a Fortune 500 company—a supersophisticated high-tech company. He started to tell me about how the organization works, how the business operates. And he told me, 'We have a nice PR group, but we should be more proactive with the press. We're responding all the time, not taking the initiative.' And I asked him, 'Okay, proactive—but to what end? What do you want to accomplish?' He looked at me and said, 'You know, nobody really ever asked me that; I don't know.'"

The short answer is simple: you want to advance your corporate strategy, to put across specific messages for specific business reasons. Every company needs a media plan, a plan that says: These are our business objectives. We intend to measure them with these benchmarks. To make it all happen, we'll have to convince these groups to take this set of actions. And this is how we'll reach them.

A communications strategy is targeted communication with a bottom-line objective. To build it, you answer a few questions.

First, what are your company's objectives? You can start with any clearly articulated business goal from the company's strategic plan. Perhaps it's to reposition the company or increase market share. Maybe you're a Woolworth's that would like to get out of the five-and-dime business. Maybe you're a Cohen's Optical that wants to go global or a Microsoft that wants to expand its presence in the word-processing field.

These are clear-cut objectives. General promotion is not. Therefore, getting lots of favorable publicity is not an appropriate goal in a media plan. Nor is seeking press coverage for the introduction of a new sports car or film or screwdriver. That's product promotion, not a strategy. The media plan needs to be just as broad based, multidimensional, and long term as the corporate strategic plan. "An awful lot of companies are very confused," said Kekst. "They jump to the conclusion that the purpose of media relations is to get good publicity for themselves or their products. They see it as a cheap way of getting advertising. But the point is not to get publicity. It's to win constituent support."

Once your objectives are identified, the next question is, Who's my audience? The query is not as simplistic as it seems. Every mass-market communication reaches multiple audiences. When you give a newspaper interview, you are talking to many constituencies at once: your customers, suppliers, employees, board of directors, shareholders, and your community, state, and national representatives—even your competitors. What plays well with one group may not with others. This is a realization that, while obvious, reaches some chastened CEOs too late. In the 1970s, for example, the same message that helped IBM sell its products—touting Big Blue's size and market strength—was also ammunition for the Department of Justice in its antitrust suit against the company.

Sometimes the same corporate action can be played as two different messages to two different audiences. For example, when semiconductor giant Intel Corporation teamed up with Sharp Electronics in 1992 to manufacture flash memory, an energy-efficient computer chip that may eventually eliminate disk drives, it was concerned about the fallout. "We didn't want a story that read, 'Another leading U.S. technology company giving away its technology to the Japanese,'" recalled Howard High, media-relations manager of Intel. "For U.S. reporters we emphasized that this was a product invented by the Japanese that had been a commercial success for an American company, and that we needed a lot of manufacturing capability to maintain our number-one market position. We also told reporters that the partnership was an opportunity for America to penetrate the Japanese market." Japan received a different message: "Over there we emphasized the partnership as a way to ease tensions and break down barriers between the countries," said High. The result was dozens of favorable front-page write-ups in both countries and a glowing piece on ABC's *World News Tonight*.

To advance your goals, you probably need the support of at least one key constituency. Once you identify it you can target your message. For example:

• You're a pharmaceutical company like Pfizer or Merck trying to put your products on the market more quickly, but you're hobbled by government bureaucracy. Testing could keep your drugs out of the stores for years. Your audience: the Food and Drug Administration.

• You're a clothing manufacturer known for cheap jeans. You want to move into the upscale market. You need to change your image from budget to big dollars. Your audience: the high-end consumer.

• You're an engineering firm whose stock price is falling because shareholders don't think you have a future. In fact, you've invested heavily in R&D that will bear fruit in the next few years. Your audience: security analysts and shareholders.

• You're a movie studio seeking to improve your releases over the next three years. In the mid-'80s, Paramount Pictures decided to do just that. Its first step toward quality lay in recruiting more talented producers and directors. So Paramount set out to create an impression of a thriving, imaginative, and supportive workplace. Its audience: top creative talent.

We have barely touched on the most important audience of all: your employees. Increasing efficiency and productivity is a long-range goal of just about any organization. The key audience for that message is employees. "That's a big issue," said Grant N. Horne, vice-president of corporate communications for Pacific Gas and Electric Company, based in San Francisco. "There's nothing like media to get the employees to buy in. If you get on the cover of *Fortune*, you must be doing something right. There's more immediate buy-in from that than from all the face-to-face meetings you hold." Media attention helps employees feel that the company is moving in the right direction, Horne continued. "That gets them motivated."

Once the media strategist has isolated his goal, his audience, and the type of message he wants to get across, he asks the final question: In what ways can I communicate my message?

"We do a cost-benefit analysis of every interview request, every speaking engagement request," said John Onoda, vice-president of corporate communications at clothing giant Levi Strauss, also based in San Francisco. "We look at what the opportunities are to present our message, how it fits into the company's business strategy and the desire to provide leadership. We say, 'Here are six messages we're concerned about. Here's how we can advance them by picking forum X, declining forum Y.'"

When P. Roy Vagelos, CEO of Merck, appeared on ABC's *This Week With David Brinkley* in March 1993, he had a specific message for a specific audience. With the pharmaceutical industry under attack for price-gouging, he needed to assert that drug prices are reasonable given high research costs. His audience was Congress, which was preparing to debate President Clinton's health-care package, a package that might include pharmaceutical cost-fixing.

PETER UEBERROTH SAW HIS NEW CITATION CABIN ON THIS SCREEN FOUR MONTHS BEFORE IT WAS ACTUALLY BUILT.

When entrepreneur Peter Ueberroth came to Cessna to select his new interior, we showed him hundreds of beautiful fabric and hardwood options. Moments later, we showed him something even better – a realistic simulation of his Citation cabin, with all his choices "installed."

This computer visualization system is just one of many surprising innovations at Cessna's new Customer Center. And it's one reason why our owners face no surprises at all when their Citations are completed.

THE SENSIBLE CITATIONS

Cessna
A Textron Company

By defining your goal, your audience, and your message, you arrive at a media plan, a blueprint that will define your interactions with the press. Of course, not every media encounter will fit your blueprint, but at least you'll have mapped out a set of principles and a sense of direction. You will have prepared your company to take an activist role, and everyone will be working from the same set of concepts.

In 1992 American Brands, the big consumer products conglomerate based in Old Greenwich, Connecticut, undertook an interesting and potentially risky shift in tactics. Many pundits were speculating that as consumers began to drink and smoke less during the coming years, their choice would be higher quality brands at higher prices. But American Brands chose to buck conventional wisdom. "In the 1990s, we feel that consumers will want price value," said CEO William Alley. "That's part of the operational strategy going through all our companies." Alley set out to get this low-cost, best-buy message across to financial analysts and consumers. He laid the groundwork at a consumer-stock analysts meeting, where he reported that alcohol and tobacco customers were looking for bargains. He was trying to plant a new idea with the shapers of public opinion. Then Alley turned to the press. "When I agreed to talk for an article in *Fortune*," he recalled, "our point was to talk about price value. That was our objective."

In the July '92 article, "How to Win With a Value Strategy," *Fortune* quoted Alley in a tidy news bite: "Value is in, ostentation is out." Even better were the quotations from industry consultants. "American Brands is doing a terrific job of convincing the public that its main-line liquors are just as good as prestige ones," said Tom Pirko, a beverage-industry analyst. The article included a chart listing the company's 1991 net profits— $830.5 million, up 34.5 percent since 1990.

Alley had created a budget-buying trend and positioned himself and his company at its head. American Brands wasn't simply trying to sell its products; it was selling itself as part of a larger movement sweeping America. That was a much more exciting, newsworthy story and more powerful as a sales tool. And in fact recent cuts in product prices by RJR Nabisco and Philip Morris have validated Alley's prediction.

When CEO William Alley chose a risky "best-buy" strategy for American Brands, he gave interviews positioning the company at the head of a trend sweeping America. Above, Alley installs a new company product.

◆

Unocal faced a different challenge through the 1980s. Like most energy companies, it labored under public skepticism, even hostility, on environmental issues. Moreover, it was stymied by what CEO Richard Stegemeier termed the "technological strait-jacket" of regulation. The company found itself spending more than $300 million a year—nearly twice what it paid shareholders in dividends—just to comply with environmental legislation. Stegemeier wasn't doubting the need for clean air and water; he just felt that the private sector could come up with solutions that were both cheaper for business and more effective in cleaning up the environment than the narrow government regulations. Stegemeier and his team launched an attack on two fronts: to simultaneously raise Unocal's environmental image and to change regulations. His audience was his community and his legislators.

In June 1990 Unocal began the South Coast Recycled Auto

Project (SCRAP). Over four months the company bought more than 8,000 pre-1971 cars from individual California car owners. Unocal's point: By junking older, less fuel-efficient cars, it could significantly reduce air pollution. Through the SCRAP program, Unocal prevented nearly 13 million pounds of pollutants from reaching the Southern California skies.

This good corporate citizenship improved Unocal's environmental image. But it had a subtler point as well. "It cost us $6 million," said Stegemeier, "and it removed as much pollution from the air as we could have by spending 10 times as much to modify one of our refineries." The message to the community was: Get the regulators off our backs, and we'll give you more inventive, cost-effective solutions that are better for the environment and better for business. As consumers, you won't be hit with the higher expenses of pass-along cost increases, and you'll still get the ecological results you're after.

"The shareholders asked, 'Why should we spend $6 million on this? Why don't we increase dividends?' But this is our strategy," said Stegemeier, "and we're doing it for a reason. If we can get away from regulations, if the government will let us spend one-half as much to do twice as much for the environment, it ought to be beneficial to society and to our bottom line."

Stegemeier's strategy garnered Unocal five and a half months of publicity. It brought national and international exposure. Best of all, in March 1992 President Bush called for a national "cash for clunkers" program modeled on SCRAP.

SCRAP won Unocal community respect, the praise of environmental groups, and the President's Environment and Conservation Challenge Award. And the long-term results may be even more encouraging. SCRAP appears to have pushed regulators to consider market-driven measures that would allow Unocal and other companies to meet their environmental obligations in more creative, less expensive ways.

The stories of American Brands and Unocal show the kind of victories that can be won by focusing on single issues. The next step is to weave several key issues into a broad-based media plan. The story of Federal Express is one such example.

Let's say it's the spring of 1973 and you're CEO Frederick W. Smith trying to get Federal Express off the ground. Airports

Unocal chief executive Richard Stegemeier set out both to repair the energy company's poor public image and to loosen environmental regulations by launching the 1990 SCRAP program. He holds some crushed metal, remnants of the heavily polluting cars destroyed by the program.

◆

don't want your planes, regulators are giving you a hard time, and consumers don't even know they want your service. You're losing money—more than $1 million a month. You're stuck with a federal regulation that prohibits cargo planes from carrying more than 6,000 pounds per load. In other words, you have to buy three small planes because you're not allowed to fill one 727.

Your audience is the bureaucrats at the Federal Aviation Administration, and your message is that small-minded regulations are stifling trade and holding back the growth of American business. You also have to compete with the U.S. Postal Service. You want to reinforce doubts about the U.S. mail by fostering any article that says the post office is inefficient or unreliable. And you want targeted publicity for your new system. You want your name recognized and associated with one or two key themes like innovation and reliability. In what ways, other than advertising, do you get this message out?

One way is with stories. At Federal Express they tell of one employee, the manager of a remote station in the California mountains. When a howling blizzard knocked out the telephone lines, the manager lost contact with his couriers. The repair company said it would take three to four days to reconnect the lines. Not even a four-wheel-drive could get through. So the manager chartered a helicopter and flew to the scene of the damaged relays. But the helicopter couldn't land. The intrepid manager had the pilot fly low, shimmied down a rope, and jumped. He then slogged through waist-deep snow, climbed the tower, and fixed the relays himself—all to be sure that the packages would arrive on time.

Maybe it's an apocryphal story, maybe not. But this story and others like it epitomize the message Federal Express most wants the public to hear. And it does what the stories behind a media strategy should do: it solidifies the company's reputation and persuades its constituencies to react, and consequently act, in the company's favor.

OF ALL THE SOPHISTICATED TOOLS USED TO BUILD CITATION BUSINESS JETS, THIS ONE IS THE MOST IMPORTANT.

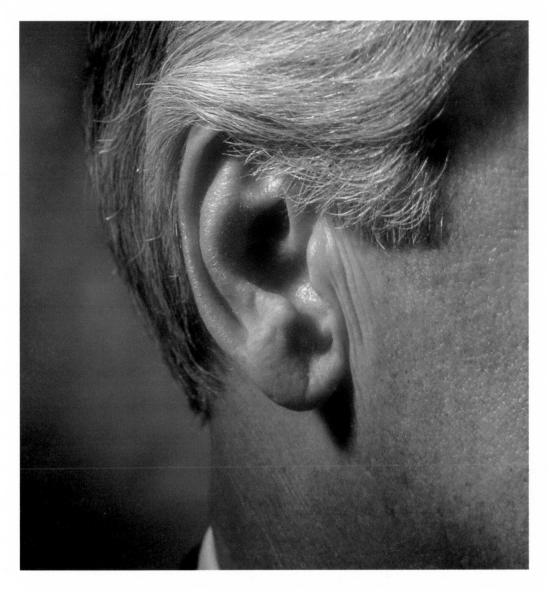

Among the many individuals and forums we listen to at Cessna is an independent group of pilots and maintenance experts we call our Advisory Council. On the new Citation X they said, "Give us a 320-kt climb speed, wider baggage door and easy avionics access." So we did. Along with hundreds of other things to make our Citations the best they can possibly be for the people who use them. It's really not very complicated how we know precisely what Citation operators want and need in their aircraft. We simply ask them.

THE SENSIBLE CITATIONS

Cessna
A Textron Company

Chapter Four

THE STORY

We can talk about communication strategies, we can talk about media plans, but at the heart of any company's future lies the CEO's vision—a vision that's the basis for the strategic plan and the core of all corporate communication. "This is my company," says the chief executive, "and this is where it's going." The CEO is weaving a narrative of his company and its destiny that he hopes will inspire his workers, catch the eye of a story-hungry media, and capture the public's imagination.

Developing such a vision may sound easy, but for many CEOs, stepping beyond the minutiae of day-to-day operations, beyond this quarter's returns and next quarter's projections, is extremely difficult. Most find it hard to focus on the horizon instead of the fires at their feet.

"It's a great weakness in American business," said Gershon Kekst. "Ask CEOs, 'How do you define your company? What's your strategic vision? How are you different from everybody else?' You can get them to describe their corporate culture but not what values they stand for. The norm is that most companies have not figured it out. They don't know."

Presidents Franklin Roosevelt (left), Ronald Reagan (center), and Bill Clinton all knew how to use stories and symbols to build popular support. Roosevelt captivated millions with his fireside chats. Reagan projected himself as America's heartland cowboy. And saxman Clinton won the 1992 election by aligning himself with youth, change, and the common folk.

◆

Greg LaBrache, senior vice-president and director of media relations at Hill & Knowlton, has seen vivid demonstrations of this shortsightedness: "I've been approached by executives from aerospace and heavy manufacturing firms who say, 'Get us favorable coverage. We'll pay you, no matter what, just get us favorable coverage.' So I say, 'Okay, what story do you have to tell?' And you know, they haven't even thought about it."

Kekst begins the search for story by asking CEOs four questions. They generally have no trouble with the first: What economic levers will propel earnings growth for your company? The next three are harder: Who are you as a company? What do you do for a living? What do you want to become?

If you can't answer these questions right away, don't be surprised. After all, George Bush lost the 1992 election at least partly because he couldn't answer questions like these, because he lacked "the vision thing." Bush had a distinguished resume, even a caring character, but he had no story to tell. Bill Clinton, on the other hand, may have had shortcomings, but he had a story, a story of youth and change. He represented a new generation appealing to common people with economic woes. Every campaign image tied into that story—dancing to Fleetwood Mac at the convention, Aretha Franklin singing "The Star Spangled Banner," even the cross-country bus trip.

Successful political leaders are among the best storytellers. Franklin Roosevelt was a storyteller; so was Ronald Reagan. And as business becomes more visible, more publicly accountable in areas once considered the politician's domain—the environment, the community, the economy—business leaders too will have to understand how to reach the public through storytelling.

The reason many Americans often don't understand business—a frequent complaint from executives—is that business and the public are not speaking the same language. Business uses terms like *P/E ratios*, *P&L statements*, and *earnings per share*. It doesn't converse through stories and characters, despite their appeal to a mass audience. "You can talk about microns till the cows come home," said Howard High of Intel, "but how much better to say a chip is as thin as a human hair." Even for the hardened business reader, financial data are most powerfully communicated when told in human terms. Readers and viewers may be interested in numbers, but they are captivated by stories.

So too are the employees. It's not the ledger that motivates them, it's the dream of where the company is heading. Professors Gary Hamel of the London Business School and C. K. Prahalad of the University of Michigan described this phenomenon under the rubric "strategic intent" in a 1989 issue of the *Harvard Business Review*: "Ask the chairmen of many American corporations how they measure their contributions to their companies' success, and you're likely to get an answer expressed in terms of shareholder wealth. It is hard to imagine middle managers, let alone blue-collar employees, waking up each day with the sole thought of creating more shareholder wealth. But mightn't they feel different given the challenge to 'Beat Benz'—the rallying cry at one Japanese auto producer?" Hamel and Prahalad are talking about the use of vision as story: We are the company that will knock off Mercedes-Benz; you and I are going to work hard over the next three years and our cars will outrun and outsell Mercedes.

Stories communicate the essence of what you are about, what you aspire to be as an organization. The vision may sometimes seem vague, but the stories are concrete. For example, you may see your company becoming your industry's premier customer-service organization. But your vision becomes much more tangible if you illustrate it with a tale of an employee who worked 53 hours straight to craft a glass chandelier and then drove from Boston to Philadelphia to hand-deliver the fragile piece to a customer. Such a story makes your vision real.

So how do you form a vision for your company? Just as the media strategy is derived point by point from your strategic plan, your vision should emerge from your company's core values, its mission statement. Said Greg LaBrache, "Start with your goals—to be known as the volume leader, or whatever—and work backwards." According to John Onoda of Levi's, "Every company has a personality, just as people do. It's simply a question of bringing it into focus."

"Companies are often unaware of their own stories," said LaBrache. "'Oh, yeah,' they'll say, 'our engineers are turning lead into gold.' They may know that, but the world out there doesn't." By focusing on the narratives that are part of your company's tradition, by putting into words what you have been trying to accomplish, you often arrive at the vision.

In 1962 Avis Rent-A-Car turned second place into a victory with its motto, "We're number two; we try harder." Avis was the home of the little guy, the underdog. When employees bought the company in a 1987 stock-option purchase, Avis's theme meshed perfectly with the news of the buyout: the little guys, the employees who tried harder, were buying the firm and leading it into the future. The company reaped a PR bonanza. "When we became employee-owned, it was a major press event," said CEO Joseph V. Vittoria, "a national event. We had a clear story to tell, and the same things that made the employee buyout work for the company made it work as a story."

In 1991 Microsoft needed another kind of tale. The company looked at competitors such as WordPerfect and Lotus and set a goal: to be a leader in word-processing and spreadsheet software within two years. But it faced an image problem. *Microsoft's products are too complicated*, said the customers. *The engineers work with their backs to us.* Microsoft needed to emphasize how easy their products were to use. So it began telling stories about its devel-

Avis CEO Joseph Vittoria capital-ized on the 1987 employee buyout by perceiving its link to the company's theme of trying harder.

opment laboratories, where managers tested their products on potential customers.

The stories were not always flattering to Microsoft's staff. Often they featured software engineers presenting hot ideas for new products like Microsoft Excel, the versatile spreadsheet software, only to be shaken by the man-on-the-street response. For example, as Microsoft's confident programmers tested the new software, they were shocked by the customers' confused reactions to the system's prompting questions. According to Marty Taucher, Microsoft's director of public relations, "The customers just humiliated these guys. The development managers were so sure that the prompting questions were obvious. But they sure weren't obvious to the users. 'It can't be that hard,' our programmers said at first. Finally they said, 'Well, I guess we'll have to rethink them.'"

These stories played well in the media. "The press loves that human-interest element—that you're willing to admit mistakes, that you learn," said Taucher. "It helps your credibility." Microsoft's willingness to humble itself, to tell stories of failures, helped convince the public that easy-to-use products were important to the company too.

At McDonald's the stories have focused on the company's competitive philosophy embodied in the sayings of the late chairman Roy Kroc. "If my competitor was drowning," he'd say, "I'd put a hose in his mouth." Cutthroat competition is the company's credo, even after hours. Every year CEO Michael R. Quinlan invites select company executives to an all-night poker game, a macho riverboat-style event. But it's more than just a game. It represents the way McDonald's wants to do business. It says: In a trade where profit margins are pennies and competitors are legion, we compete from corner to corner, from street to street, minute by minute all across the world. In short, the poker game has become a company symbol.

A symbol is simply the company's vision distilled to one key image. But that image can be powerful in the media because it defines and dominates the debate; it lingers when everything else is forgotten. The Unocal SCRAP program was effective because it offered a highly visual symbol: a junker car dragged into a scrapyard and put under the crusher.

An equally potent automotive metaphor was born early in 1990, Saturn's first year of business, when this supposedly different car company turned out 1,800 vehicles with faulty coolants. Instead of equivocating or recalling the cars for lengthy repairs, the company replaced them. It was a powerful reminder that Saturn believes its cars should be perfect. The company can turn out as many ads as it wants, but this one action was the perfect media symbol—sending out a loud message that Saturn values its customers and acts accordingly. Saturn repeated the message in August 1993, when a wiring difficulty prompted a recall of 352,767 cars. Saturn contacted all the customers affected, arranging barbecues, movies, and free transportation for those faced with a repair delay.

Of course, symbols can also work negatively. Some decisions carry potentially damaging symbolic freight, and obvious gaffes slip by even the biggest companies. For instance, in 1986 General Motors laid off thousands of employees, at the same time promising a $2.2 million bonus to then CEO Roger B. Smith. And when it comes to environmental issues, so often imbued with emotion, a huge symbolic weight is attached to the smallest matters. You may try to convince the public that a ratio of two parts pollutant per million of clean air is negligible, but no one will believe you. Those invisible particles will hover in the mind's eye like a million parts per million. Trying to convince people otherwise, says William Sprague of Savannah Foods—a master of the symbolic—"well, it's like pissing into a hurricane."

SCHEDULE A BUSINESS MEETING
NEXT DOOR TO THE SOUND BARRIER.

Inside, it is an elegant conference room. Quiet. Abundantly spacious. Beautifully appointed. With soft leather recliners, individual television monitors, and a private dressing room.

Outside, it is slicing through the sky at more than 870 feet per second. Mach .90. One-tenth of a point below the speed of sound.

The remarkable new Citation X. Reservations will be accepted soon for demonstration flights in 1995. And they'll be going fast.

THE SENSIBLE CITATIONS

Chapter Five

PUTTING IT ALL TOGETHER: TWO CASE STUDIES

A prime example of an integrated media plan can be found at Levi Strauss. Levi's is the largest branded apparel company in the world, but when it comes to communications, its focus is not on size or industry dominance. You'll rarely hear talk about Levi Strauss going eyeball to eyeball with competitors until one or the other blinks. Instead, the company defines itself through another theme: progressiveness.

The story workers tell at Levi's took place in the mid-1980s. A group of employees went to CEO Robert D. Haas, and the gist of their message was, "This company is not so great for women and minorities." Haas was startled but replied, "Let's talk about it." At a follow-up corporate retreat, the senior managers (almost all of them white males) met with the group. There a facilitator asked both the senior managers and the other employees to write a brief description of life for women and minorities at Levi Strauss. The managers wrote statements such as, "Things are great. We're on the cutting edge. The number of women and minority employees at Levi's is higher than at most other companies." The descriptions written by women and minorities said, in essence, "Things are not great. There's racism, sexism, a double standard, and a glass ceiling."

"It was like night and day," said John Onoda, vice-president of corporate communications. "The two groups looked across the room and saw this huge gulf. Following the meeting, the company drew up a set of aspirations. We were determined to show we listen to people." Over the following years the company responded by instituting companywide forums on diversity, including a three-day course for managers, as well as support networks and career development courses for various ethnic groups.

The story of that initial retreat has been told many times internally and published in the *Harvard Business Review*. It has come to define Levi Strauss as a company so determined to be enlightened and progressive that it's ready to take its lumps for not being progressive enough.

How did Haas and others at Levi's integrate this story into a media strategy, and more important, what is its business value? Clearly such advanced policies give the company an image as a leader. For example, Haas has spoken out forcefully and often in speeches and in magazines such as *Business Week* about the importance of work-force diversity. As indicated in "Workforce 2000," a 1987 study published by the Hudson Institute, the mix in the American workplace will change radically over the coming years. "Only 15 percent of the entry workers will be white males," said Onoda. "You know, if you're a CEO 15 years from now, you're going to have a very different work force. So how do you recruit the most talented minorities? You do it by speaking out on diversity. That's how they'll remember you when they ask, 'Where can I advance? Where is skin color not an issue?' They'll come to you. That's a big business benefit."

Levi Strauss is so committed to fostering an atmosphere of nondiscrimination that it's taken some controversial stands, understanding their symbolic weight. When the Boy Scouts stated that they would not accept avowed homosexuals and atheists as scouts or scout leaders, Levi's withdrew financial support, saying it would not give to any organization that discriminated. This willingness to take a public stand on social issues is part of the company's long-term strategic thinking, said Onoda: "It's the cultural spine of the company—qualities you can't measure in dollars and cents." By consolidating story, strategy, and symbol, Levi's is working with a unified media plan.

For Pacific Gas and Electric, the media challenge was more acute: how to overcome a poor environmental image. In one of the most heavily regulated industries, this reputation stood a good chance of blocking development.

The problem peaked in the late '80s, as PG&E was constructing its controversial Diablo Canyon nuclear-power plant just five miles from a fault line in Southern California. As engineering flaws turned up during construction and the licensing procedure dragged on, building costs rose, costs that ratepayers would ultimately bear. When the company tried to recover $7 billion from the public, the community was outraged. Regulators disallowed most of the expenses, saying the company would have to swallow $4 billion of the costs. PG&E engineers urged litigation to recover the money, stating that the flaws fell within the declared tolerances of the design specifications required by the Nuclear Regulatory Commission. The engineers felt certain that PG&E would win any lawsuit.

But CEO Richard A. Clarke realized that he might win the financial battle but lose the media war, a war that could drag on, souring the public's view of PG&E, depressing the share price, and stalling the company's future. Rather than tough it out, he brought in negotiator Warren Christopher. Christopher, who subsequently became Bill Clinton's secretary of State, managed a settlement that whittled the $4 billion down to $1 billion, and PG&E took a highly publicized write-off. Bad news? Not really, said Grant Horne: "As a media strategy, we actually wanted the headlines that said PG&E TAKES $1 BILLION HIT FOR ALLEGED PROBLEMS. That was superb. We needed to get the negative news out. People needed to see the company experience pain." It sounds a little strange, but Horne was clear on the motivation. "Until the public sees you've paid," he said, "you're not going to get anywhere—not with the public, not with the consumers. You have to bring the issue to closure."

There were still lingering doubts, however, about PG&E's trustworthiness. Would the company be prepared to close down the plant if it needed repairs? Would PG&E swallow the

To dispel mounting public distrust over the construction of one of Pacific Gas and Electric's nuclear-power plants, chief executive Richard Clarke encouraged a highly publicized $1 billion write-off. Above, Clarke stands in front of a waterfall at company headquarters.

◆

$4-million-a-day cost of a shutdown? Or would it just cover up potential problems? So Horne and Clarke came up with a powerful symbol—a 24-hour 800-number that area residents could call to voice concerns about safety or to ask questions. "Some people say it's a waste of money," said Horne. "I don't think so. People want the reassurance. It's a credibility matter."

Symbols don't always correlate with reality. After all, would an 800-number help in the event of a nuclear catastrophe? Not really. You'd be glowing in the dark before you dialed the first digit. But that's not the point. The point is to communicate a particular message to win over a key constituency. Publicity about the 800-number has done that handsomely.

PG&E's improved media image as an environmentally conscientious company created other benefits for the company as well. PG&E recently looked at California's energy needs for the next decade and projected it would have to raise $4 billion to build new plants. Environmental groups objected, asserting that three-quarters of California's growing energy demand could be handled by conservation. But even if they were right, how would PG&E make money? With the Sierra Club and the Environmental Defense Fund, groups that had once looked on the company as "the enemy," PG&E came up with a unique plan—a proposal that would guarantee PG&E a $2 billion profit from a schedule of rate increases over several years. The profit would come not from creating new energy or new plants but from fostering conservation. By offering public education, residential insulation programs, as well as financial incentives to industry, PG&E estimated it could in fact cut new energy demand by 75 percent over the next decade. Consumers would save 50 percent, spending $2 billion instead of $4 billion; the shareholders would make $45 million; PG&E would get its profit; and the environment would benefit.

Best of all, the environmental groups did all the lobbying, winning over the press, the regulators, and the public to PG&E's cause. What more can you ask for from a media plan?

FLIES LIKE A JET.
BUYS LIKE A TURBOPROP.

From the moment the first CitationJet took flight, the rules were changed forever. Cruising at 437 mph, the CitationJet is the first business jet that significantly outperforms ordinary turboprops at a guaranteed lower operating cost, *and* costs far less to purchase.

The technological advancements engineered into this extraordinary aircraft mean that even with a smaller price tag, the CitationJet has a great number of things the turboprop does not. Including a bright future.

THE SENSIBLE CITATIONS

Cessna
A Textron Company

Chapter Six

MEET THE PRESS

ny CEO planning to expand into a foreign country would undoubtedly do market research first. In many ways, the press *is* a foreign country. Its customs and traditions are different from corporate America's. And to put it bluntly, when it comes to the media many business executives are wandering around without a map. "I'm amazed how little they understand the press," said one journalist. "A lot of them don't have a clue."

On the flip side, the majority of journalists are not experts in business and finance. "Most reporters are not that well informed, especially at the local newspapers," said James Smith of First American. "And when you talk to TV reporters, forget it. They don't understand half the issues." Richard Stegemeier of Unocal agreed: "The press is not well enough educated, especially on the technical side. As an engineer, I have to chuckle at some of what I read."

Even as the press gets more sophisticated about business, and vice versa, a gulf remains. A 1992 Harris Survey on the quality of business journalism in America shows the disparity: 79 percent of reporters but only 54 percent of executives gave business journalists a favorable rating. And 84 percent of reporters polled considered themselves "fair, balanced, and accurate." Just 27 percent of the executives agreed.

Whether they'll say it for the record or not, many business leaders believe the press is unbalanced, biased, and too liberal. Some CEOs claim the media, even *The Wall Street Journal*, are anti-business. The feeling is that the press is not out to report the facts but to dig up the dirt on corporate America. "Ever since Watergate," said William Alley of American Brands, "the desire for a Pulitzer, for exposure, or to find something dire, something that will sell publications, has driven journalists towards investigative reporting rather than straightforward journalism."

Reporters disagree. "It's the same aggressive reporting that's been focused on political issues for years, now being focused on business issues," said Janet Guyon of *The Wall Street Journal*, "and executives are just not used to it. But that's a permanent change."

Actually, if you pick up any paper and count the pages devoted to business, you'll see that the majority of business column inches are not dedicated to attacks or praise but to neutral information such as earnings reports.

Most of the time business gets the press it deserves, commented one AT&T executive. "When we start doing better, our coverage will get better." Stephen B. Shepard, editor in chief of *Business Week*, put it another way: "Business coverage is like sports coverage. There are numbers to look at. Either a guy has a good batting average or he doesn't. Either the car sells or it doesn't. Most of the time the results are objectively measurable."

In the end, how you judge the press isn't really so important. For the realist, the issue is more basic: the media aren't going anywhere. They'll be here tomorrow and the next day. So how can you work with them? How can you make them work for you? You've developed a media plan and shaped a message. Now how do you get it across?

Let's start with an obvious point, but one that bears repeating: Reporters are beyond your control. That's what it means to have a free press. And that's the uncertain situation of an executive facing the media. There's no way to ensure that your story will get picked up or, if it is, that it won't get mangled. But the smart CEO finds subtle ways to improve the odds. He knows that all he needs is a little edge.

The first questions to ask are, Who are these reporters, anyway, and what drives them? They are, after all, the means of delivery for your message. As monolithic as the press might appear from the outside, it is in fact more Balkanized than the Balkans. There are so many news organizations with so many different agendas and deadlines: print and electronic media, local and national, daily, weekly, and monthly. Many executives have become sophisticated enough to go beyond the organization to the individual, to realize there's not so much a *Los Angeles Times* or *Washington Post* "take" on a story as a reporter A or a reporter B take. The more you know about the reporters on your beat, the more you can speak their language and put your story across in the most effective way.

Moreover, journalists have a different ethos, a different way of working than corporate America. A story about *Wall Street Journal* reporter Kevin Salwen illustrates the point. Salwen had written a few articles about the Securities and Exchange Commission that Richard C. Breeden, its chairman from 1989 to 1993, had perceived as unflattering. When Salwen looked into the chairman's allegedly overdue membership fee at a Washington club, Breeden was so infuriated he called bureau chief Al Hunt to complain. Then one of Salwen's friends at the SEC pulled him aside: "You'd better watch out," he said. "Breeden is on the warpath." Salwen was unperturbed. "No," his friend said, "You don't understand. He's going to make trouble with your boss." Salwen smiled. "*You* don't understand," he said. "This is the best thing that could happen to me. My boss is now talking to me all the time, patting me on the back."

Unless reporters stir up trouble and get people mad from time to time, their bosses don't think they're doing their job. This is the opposite of the corporate "cover your ass" credo.

Many chief executives see the press as an extension of their marketing arm. Their top PR officials frequently come from marketing. The general corporate approach is summed up by the president of one East Coast energy company. "Frankly," he said, "our management just wants to issue press releases and see them printed in the paper." But this approach doesn't work. No self-respecting reporter will copy down a release and issue it as gospel. Nevertheless, major companies consistently seem to believe that's just what reporters will do. "Companies often assume their version is the only version," said Stephen Shepard of *Business Week*. "They say, 'Why didn't you print what we told you?' Well, they have a point of view. But regulators, analysts, their competitors—they all have other points of view."

Laura Landro, media and marketing editor of *The Wall Street Journal*, agreed. "The main problem with CEOs, even the most savvy, is that they literally cannot understand. They say, 'I had you here in my office, I spent my valuable time, I told you everything was great. Why didn't you print what I told you?' I can't count how many times that's happened."

Paul B. Carroll, another *Wall Street Journal* reporter, gives an example from his years covering IBM: "The company held a meeting to discuss job cuts and to describe how all the problems had now been taken care of. I went back and wrote a page-one story about how IBM had caused all the problems and layoffs in the first place by creating a price war it couldn't win. The head of PR called me up and said, 'What I don't understand is, what meeting is it you covered?' And I told her, 'Just because you hold a meeting doesn't mean I have to write about it. Just because you have a message doesn't mean I have to write about it.' To this day, she hasn't gotten it. Her problem is, she views me as the *Wall Street Journal* manager on the IBM account."

Just as strong as your instinct to manage the press is a reporter's need to apply his own intelligence when writing a story. This is not necessarily bias or muckraking. It's just not the same old Chamber of Commerce puff pieces. Business journalism has become more discerning.

The media's agenda is not your agenda. But they need you to fill their columns, their air time. And, of course, you need them if you care whether anyone ever hears of your company. In short, business and the media are stuck with each other. But the press is not the enemy. You and the media have a relationship. And like any relationship, you have to work on it to make it livable.

The smart CEO sets out to forge a long-term partnership between his company and the press. Like rapport with customers or suppliers, this relationship is built on trust and understanding. You build it by being accessible and frank. The press builds it by being accurate and fair.

Many CEOs probably hope reporters like them and their staffs, expecting that journalist friends will not write negative stories. But reporters are there to do a job and tell the story as they see it. The goal of this relationship is not the slender reed of friendship but education. You want the reporters covering you to understand your company and industry and the context in which you make decisions. The more they grasp your point of view, the more they will do it justice. That's why instead of complaining about the lack of educated reporters, most Fortune 500 CEOs and their top managers—from Robert L. Crandall, CEO of American Airlines, and John F. Welch Jr., CEO of General Electric, to John Sculley, chairman of Apple, and Andrew S. Grove, CEO of Intel—have "background" lunches from time to time with the editorial boards and the beat reporters of major magazines and newspapers. Over soup and salad and salmon, they hold roundtable discussions, briefing the press on industry developments. Other executives meet with their local news editors and reporters. One way or another, you have to have contact if you're going to develop a relationship.

Establishing this partnership does not mean you are going to do everything the press wants. As CEO you have more on your plate than picking up the phone every time a reporter calls or acceding to every media request. "We're not going to put our heads in a revolving door just to see what happens," said Robert J. Rukeyser, senior vice-president of corporate affairs at American Brands.

If one basic rule applies, however, it's that you should talk—not as a favor to the press but as a favor to yourself. Otherwise everyone else—the regulators or your competitors or your customers—will dominate the public dialogue about your company. "If you don't position yourself," said Marty Taucher of Microsoft, "others will do it for you." Or as Bob Crandall is fond of saying, "Unless we sit down and talk, we don't have a chance to get across our point of view."

Certain CEOs make a fundamental mistake. Because they've been burned once or twice, they opt out of a relationship with the media. If they can't have control, they'd rather remain silent. What they don't understand is that only by talking do they exert some control, even in a negative piece. They may not like the final piece, but if they talk, at least they are doing what they can to get their side of the story heard.

"If the CEO wants to talk, I've got to report what he says. That's my job," said one *New York Times* reporter. "And when CEOs talk to me, they almost always get a better story from their point of view." Alecia Swasy of *The Wall Street Journal* agreed: "CEOs grossly underestimate their abilities to influence the press day in and day out. When a CEO talks, he's going to get into the article. He's going to bump other things out. I don't think they play that card often enough." And the card has another advantage as well. Every time a chief executive talks, he is also building long-term rapport with the media.

As you construct a relationship with the press, here's what it should be able to count on from you and your company:
- Occasional access to you, the CEO.
- Prompt return of phone calls by your staff.
- Respect for newspaper and TV deadlines.
- Clear, factual, and honest information.

The last point is particularly important, because reporters have long memories, and they will enjoy the opportunity to even the score if you present inaccurate or dishonest information. "CEOs have an interest in trying to manage the news," said Laura Landro. "But it's better to say nothing than lie. I'd rather have someone not return my call than lie."

Reporters aren't the only ones who should have expectations. Business can expect certain behavior from the media as well:
- Accurate reporting—no quotations mangled or taken out of context.
- An attempt to portray your side of the story.
- Fairness, which is not the same as objectivity. A good reporter is not necessarily objective. He starts with a thesis, which he will prove or disprove. But as he gathers information, he must be evenhanded and open-minded. "A good reporter is willing to listen," said Stephen Shepard. "Many times we've had a story change 180 degrees."
- Adherence to the reporter's code, which says that anything

said off the record or not for attribution stays that way. "Those promises have to be considered sacrosanct," said John Capouya, a *New York Times* editor, formerly of *New York Newsday*.

There are also a few concepts to bear in mind as you build your relationship with the media. Even if you don't want to talk about your company, you or your staff can talk about your competitors, which may further your corporate cause. Few companies do this publicly, but many will do it as an unattributed source. Said one Fortune 500 executive, "We don't want to be out there bad-mouthing the competition. But if you'll talk about another company's lousy record, if you can be used as an unattributed industry source, it not only helps your company, the reporters also appreciate it, and they don't forget that you've helped them."

You can also analyze and try to fill the media's needs. Some companies, understanding the budget constraints of TV newsgathering, supply local stations with "B-roll"—scene-setting shots—increasing the chances of getting on the air. Mazda has provided footage of its Miata sports cars, and General Electric has done the same with its factories and jet engines.

Here are a few other suggestions to think about before you talk with the press:

• Study the history of how your company and industry have been covered. If you've been shellacked on a few occasions, reporters may feel they owe you a break. It can pay to position yourself as the underdog since reporters love to take the big guy down a peg. "When T. Boone Pickens and Carl Icahn were trying to take us over," recalled Jere Smith, director of media relations at Phillips Petroleum, "we played it in the newspapers as this little company from Bartlesville, Oklahoma, under attack by these big takeover artists. Actually we were a lot bigger. But we got a lot of mileage out of being the underdog."

• Remember that most journalists appreciate humorous self-deprecation and respect someone willing to admit mistakes. And they prefer one-on-one interviews or, at most, two-on-one. Taking along four senior vice-presidents to answer every possible nuance of every question is counterproductive; reporters want the opportunity for informal conversation, especially with the CEO.

• Above all, bear in mind that reporters want a good story—

a story with tension and dramatic arc and human interest. This is the bias they have—the bias for story. Taking a big company down a notch or exposing corporate wrongdoing makes a good story. But so does the anatomy of a success or the chronology of a dramatic turnaround. Just remember to think in human terms. The evening newscast piece on unemployment, for example, will not feature a list of figures. It will highlight laid-off workers Joe and Mary Jones crying at their dining-room table.

Story is your common ground with the media. If you can think in terms of stories—of narratives, characters, and symbols—you have a much better chance of delivering your message.

TO ONE CITATION OWNER, THIS LOOKS LIKE PERFECT FLYING WEATHER.

When one University of North Dakota pilot sees a thunderhead like this, he flies directly into it. It's part of his job as a weather researcher. So far, his specially equipped Citation has carried him, his copilot, and a scientist right into the jaws of 600 severe thunderstorms. And right back out again.

It's good to know that Citations can survive rough weather, but it's better to know they don't have to. Citations are built to cruise at altitudes far above most storm clouds. And most weather researchers.

THE SENSIBLE CITATIONS

Cessna
A Textron Company

Chapter Seven

THE CRISIS

Executives have always worried about crisis. But as business has become more public, crisis control has become a crucial skill for CEOs and their staffs. How should they respond to a disaster? What if there's an explosion, a contamination, an arrest for insider trading, a major lawsuit based on fraud or embezzlement? No one wants to look like a fool in these situations. That's why even companies that lack a media plan often have a crisis-response manual. And many executive training workshops and media seminars focus on what to do when all hell breaks loose. But that emphasis is wrong.

If you have built a strong relationship with the press, if you have been frank and accessible and have taken the time to educate those on your beat, you will reap the dividends of that investment during a crisis. Not because reporters will cover for you (although they might give you the benefit of the doubt), but because you will have established your perspective; the reporters will understand the situation from your point of view.

When it comes to the extremes of managing calamity, the most familiar paradigms are Exxon and Johnson & Johnson.

In 1989 the Exxon tanker *Valdez* ran aground off the coast of Alaska and the oil started gushing. CEO Lawrence G. Rawl dithered and procrastinated and tried to play down the affair while the public howled for blood. Exxon's reputation is still tarnished.

Johnson & Johnson responded differently to the 1982 Tylenol poisoning scare. CEO James E. Burke immediately set up a communications "war room" to ensure dissemination of his story to the media. He stepped forward as a sympathetic spokesperson, expressing concern, dismay, and regret. Because of the way he handled the crisis, public confidence in J&J became stronger than ever.

Jack in the Box CEO Robert Nugent failed to accept blame for tainted meat, thus heightening the company's January 1993 crisis.

These are the textbook cases, but have their lessons been learned? In stories ranging from the 1992 Sears auto repair scandal—when Sears auto centers in several states were revealed to have charged customers for needless repairs—to Dow Corning's breast implant crisis that same year—when Dow's past failure to report the possibility of implant leakage resulted in thousands of lawsuits—corporations fell back into the same bad habits, responding to crisis with the knee-jerk "cover it up and maybe everyone will go away" response. Executives let the stories dribble out and gather a terrible momentum.

Take the tale of Jack in the Box. In January 1993 two-year-old Michael Nole ate a cheeseburger in a Tacoma, Washington, Jack in the Box. The next day he had severe stomach cramps and diarrhea. Ten days later he was dead. In all, more than 300 people throughout the West were hit by the same *E. coli* bacteria.

Foodmaker Inc., the parent company of Jack in the Box, had a crisis team that responded quickly; the restaurants threw out nearly 20,000 pounds of hamburger patties. But Foodmaker's public relations failed. For nearly a week the company made no admission of responsibility. When CEO Robert J. Nugent finally did come forward, he tried to shift the blame onto Washington State health representatives and the California-based meat supplier, the Vons Company, instead of delivering a simple, strong apology and a promise to correct the situation. By the first week in February, sales were down 40 percent.

While the company has fought back in recent months, offering to pay the medical costs of anyone harmed by the tainted meat, the lingering damage to Jack in the Box's reputation may take years to repair.

These days, disaster strikes quickly. In this age of instantaneous television reporting and electronic wire services, the CEO has to react just as quickly. Whatever the situation, the response must be immediate and straightforward. Stephen Shepard of *Business Week* has been on both the media and executive sides of crisis. "You almost always make it worse by not talking," he said. "You want to hide, but you've got to be out there. I know. When a *Business Week* radio announcer was indicted for insider trading, I wanted to go home and hide, but I had to go out there. I said, 'It's a terrible thing that's happened. We'll get to the bottom of it.' The public doesn't blame you. Your credibility doesn't suffer. One rotten apple doesn't reflect on you."

Why do so many companies choke in a crisis? The answer can be found in a CEO's typical response to disaster: damage control. It's the natural reaction to bad news. When disaster occurs, you probably find yourself in your office with two executive VPs and several lawyers, and if your company is typical, no PR executive present. The lawyers' mission is to protect you, since anything you admit may be grounds for a lawsuit. They will push hard for damage control. According to insiders, this was the situation at Exxon during the *Valdez* fiasco—the lawyers had Rawl's ear. But sometimes the public communication dimension is just as important as the legal dimension. The potential harm to consumer trust and company reputation may outweigh the risk of a suit.

As veteran listeners to after-dinner speeches may have heard, the Chinese character for crisis is composed of two joined ideograms, one representing danger, the other opportunity. It's easy to see the danger when disaster strikes. But a crisis also offers an opportunity—a better opportunity than most—to get your message across, because the press will definitely show up to cover a crisis.

So start with the rule that guides Grant Horne of Pacific Gas and Electric: "The greater the opportunity for negative news, the faster we get it out to the press in our terms." Seize the initiative. Put your message out first. And don't minimize the seriousness of the problem. When some asbestos-lined steam pipes

CESSNA HAS INVESTED A QUARTER-BILLION DOLLARS TO KEEP CITATION OPERATORS IN THEIR PLACE.

A Citation's place is in the sky. That's why every Citation is supported by the largest single-product network of any business jet in the world. Today, eight company-owned Citation Service Centers are dedicated entirely to Citations. And authorized Service Stations are located around the globe. It's a quarter-billion-dollar investment.

We figure the more we spend on the Citation service network, the less time Citation owners will spend on the ground.

THE SENSIBLE CITATIONS

Cessna
A Textron Company

burst in PG&E's electric-power plant in Carmel, California, Horne announced the problem right away. He asked his engineers, "What's the worst possible case of asbestos in the air—the very worst? Up to X parts per million? That's the number we'll give out tonight." When the actual figures came out lower, PG&E gained credibility.

Even the most media savvy, however, can miss these opportunities. When CBS anchorman Dan Rather stormed off the set in 1987 in the famous "six black minutes" affair, for example, CBS executives tried to downplay their embarrassment by covering up and lying, saying that Rather had just wandered away for a few minutes and couldn't be found. Couldn't be found? At air time? Smelling lies, the media kept pressing until the affair blew up into a scandal. CBS had had a good story to tell, if it had just played it straight. "Yes," network executives could have said, "Dan did storm off the set. He did it because coverage of a tennis match was cutting into a major news story—Pope John Paul II arriving in the United States. So for one brief moment, Dan did allow his passion for news, his commitment to excellence, to take over." Not a bad story. But instead CBS opted for damage control.

Whatever your response in a crisis, symbols heighten the impact. In January 1969 a blowout at a Unocal oil well spilled as much as 77,000 barrels of oil off the Santa Barbara coast. Eight days later Fred L. Hartley, then CEO of Unocal, testified before Senator Edmund Muskie's Public Works Committee. "I think we have to look at these problems relatively," Hartley said. "I am always tremendously impressed at the publicity that the death of birds receives versus the loss of people in our country in this day and age. When I think of the folks that gave up their lives when they came down into the ocean off Los Angeles [in a plane crash] some three weeks ago . . ." This statement got misquoted by everyone from *Time* to NBC News as, "I'm amazed at the publicity over the loss of a few birds."

For almost 25 years Unocal has been trying to straighten out that miscommunication. What the company doesn't realize is that the original is just as bad as the misquote. The symbolic weight of even one bird, covered in black, gooey oil, limping out of the surf and collapsing on the sand, is deadly. Better to create an image of your own—teams of men and women in bright white suits dispatched to combat the spill and save the birds.

In the crisis, take the focus off the damage and put it on your response—how you feel, what you are doing to combat the problem. This is what people want to know about anyway: the damage is done; now, what are you going to do about it? But it also shifts your stance—if not from villain to hero, then at least from antagonist to protagonist.

Most important, do not respond to a disaster as a business executive. Respond as a human being. In 1992, when two explosions at a Texaco oil refinery in southern Los Angeles injured 16 workers and forced 500 people from their homes, company officials tried to downplay the damage. Instead they came off sounding like automatons. How much better to say, "We're really concerned about this; we're going to do everything we can to make sure this situation is under control."

In times of trouble, people respond emotionally. If a disaster is getting major play, on page one or as the TV news lead, a large audience will be following the reports. These people do not care about P&L statements or ratio analyses or however else you measure the event. They see it in human terms. It's a story.

Imagine if your company threatened the water supply of one million people in three states, as Ashland Oil did in January 1988, when a 4-million-gallon fuel tank collapsed and contaminated two major rivers in the Pittsburgh area. Here's what Ashland did: Within 24 hours, as company workers started the cleanup, CEO John R. Hall was on the phone to state and local officials. Within 72 hours he was apologizing for the spill at an on-site press conference. He admitted his company's mistakes and submitted to tough grillings from local newspapers and TV stations. Everywhere his message was the same—contrition, concern, caring, and a willingness to pay the costs. "We are doing everything we know how to clean up the damage as rapidly as possible," he said. In an important symbolic gesture, Hall brought in independent analysts to investigate the spill. While his operating staff was working to combat the pollution, Hall was trying to combat public worries. Dan Lacy, Ashland's vice-president of corporate communications, would say later, "It's the public rather than your own operating people

By braving frigid temperatures and facing the press at the site of Ashland Oil's 1988 oil spill near Pittsburgh, chief executive John Hall helped salvage the company's image as a responsible corporate citizen.

◆

that decides how big the problem really is, in terms of public perception."

The upshot? Positive media responses. ASHLAND SCORES HIGH IN PUBLIC RELATIONS, said a *Pittsburgh Post-Gazette* headline. HONESTY ABOUT FUEL SPILL SCORES HIGH WITH THE PUBLIC, wrote *The Lexington Herald-Leader*. The article read, in part: "Ashland Oil chairman John Hall's admission that his company made mistakes in assembling the diesel fuel tank that burst last Saturday may make company attorneys wince, but his frankness is playing well in the public arena. Hall appears to be winning the confidence of government officials and the public." On the *MacNeil-Lehrer NewsHour*, an EPA official praised Ashland's actions in the spill's aftermath. Today Ashland's crisis response is studied at the Harvard Business School.

Even in the absolute worst case, two narratives remain that Americans love. The first is the triumph over adversity: the situation looked terrible, but you didn't hesitate to tackle it, and victory is now on the horizon. If you can't make that work, if things are going badly and it's all your fault, there's always the ultimate fallback—the redemption narrative. Our country's TV watchers love folks who accept the worst and turn themselves around. The airwaves are filled with reformed sinners and recovering alcoholics. They're heroes. This is their line, and you can use it too: "We bottomed out, it's true. But we worked hard, we cleaned up our act, and now we're back and better than ever." Redemption makes a great story.

THERE ARE PLENTY OF REASONS TO OWN A CITATION.
THIS ISN'T EVEN IN THE TOP TEN.

In a 1992 survey of top U.S. companies, the sales per employee for those operating aircraft were 26% greater than for those who did not. The net income was 102% greater. Financially rewarding reasons for flying one's own aircraft abound. And they are far more significant than escaping commercial airline inconvenience. There are even more reasons to make that aircraft a Citation. That's why, at 2,000 and growing, Citations form the largest fleet of business jets in the world.

THE SENSIBLE CITATIONS

Cessna
A Textron Company

Chapter Eight

LEAKS AND BAD NEWS

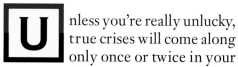nless you're really unlucky, true crises will come along only once or twice in your career. But what about those more quotidian annoyances—leaks?

The anatomy of a leak often looks like this: The staff at one major multimedia company had worked long hours to put together a hard-hitting documentary. A week before the film was to air, the CEO decided it was too abrasive and pulled it from the schedule. The staff was outraged and leaked its disapproval to the press. When the resulting news story paraded the company's internal politics, it was the CEO's turn to be outraged. He called his employees together to berate them, announcing that he'd fire anyone caught talking to the press. Then he called the newspaper and complained about having a bunch of spies in his own organization.

The upshot? The CEO looked like a fool, and the staff was livid. Even those who agreed with their boss's initial decision resented his lecturing. Several employees talked of going to the press again, just to show the CEO they couldn't be pushed around. In the end, everyone went home indignant.

These days it's almost impossible to keep a secret in a big company. Sooner or later, information almost always gets out. Too many people have too many agendas. Since the mid-'80s, old notions of loyalty have changed, due in part to restructuring and layoffs. The technology has changed too; it's now easy to intercept faxes and e-mail. And people love to talk. That's what keeps reporters in business. "It used to be hard to get leaks," remarked one reporter. "Now it's hard *not* to get leaks."

While writing a book on television news, I was told by NBC News that no one there would talk to me, that the staff had been told not to cooperate. A news organization should have known better. Within a few months I had interviewed dozens of NBC staffers—writers, producers, editors, and executives, all the way up to anchor Tom Brokaw.

Some corporations try to clamp down by intimidating their employees. The Alecia Swasy-Procter & Gamble story is not an isolated instance. When Janet Guyon of *The Wall Street Journal* published unflattering articles on AT&T in 1986, the company went through its employees' work and home phone records to find the leak. "It scared the shit out of the employees," said Guyon. "And for what? We're not talking about disclosure of any SEC or market-moving statistics here. You know, these days I'm covering Eastern Europe, and many American companies are more closed than these former communist states. They're so heavy-handed in their efforts to control information. It doesn't help the company. It creates a sense of paranoia. It just makes the reporters think something must be going on, so they dig more. And the employees get more and more disgruntled."

If you have a small company that's been ignored by the press, maybe you can clamp down on leaks for a little while. But as *Wall Street Journal* managing editor Paul Steiger put it, "When somebody closes the door, he usually looks worse." You can try to shut down, but there are always ways for the story to get out. "What companies and executives forget is that just because you don't talk doesn't mean we won't write," said Laura Landro of *The Wall Street Journal*. "There are so many sources: suppliers, reporting services, competitors, and disgruntled employees."

The realistic CEO realizes that leaks are a fact of life. "You can contain them for a while, but never totally," said Peter J. Dowd, vice-president of public relations for Texaco. What a CEO can diminish is the motivation for leaks—by working to build consensus and accord. People don't bad-mouth their company to reporters when they're happy to be on the team. "We don't have much of a problem when it comes to leaks," said C. J. "Pete" Silas, CEO of Phillips Petroleum. "We like to think it's because there's not much of a need."

Beyond the leaks, what about negative stories in general? What can be done if a news piece appears that outrages you? First, assess its accuracy. Besides what you see as misinterpretations, are the facts wrong? If so, get the correction out as soon as possible. "Once the media gets the facts wrong, it's tough to go back," said Michael W. Thacher, manager of public relations and communications for Unocal. "Things ripple out. One story gets picked up from others. The time to correct things is early—in the first few minutes or hours, if you can."

Most journalists are good about correcting factual errors. You can set the record straight with a phone call or a letter to the editor. And the majority of publications or news organizations will feel duty-bound to print or air a CEO's response. Of course, the corrections almost never get the same play as the original wrong information. Still, they can have some immediate impact, and they reduce the chances that the original error will be repeated. What does not help your cause—your long-term cause of getting good coverage over the next decade—is to overreact. Journalists take it personally when you do. As John Capouya of *The New York Times* has said in response to irate callers, "Don't try to tell me my business. I'm in the business and you're not."

When Guyon profiled General Electric CEO Jack Welch in *The Wall Street Journal* in 1988, she pointed out that he tends to blow up when crossed. Welch was steaming after he saw the piece. He sent aides to talk to Norman Pearlstine, then the *Journal's* managing editor, to demand that they "take Guyon off the company account," recalled Guyon—as if she worked for GE. "Hey," said Guyon, "I crossed him; he blew up. Was my story correct or not?"

Never try to get a reporter thrown off your beat; editors resent it, and reporters take it as a declaration of war. Most likely the reporter will stick around to haunt you and your company for a long time. And an all-out counterattack normally backfires.

Joseph Vittoria of Avis spoke of his experiences in the early 1980s: "There was this financial analyst who had a vendetta against us, and whenever anyone had a story, they went to him for a quote. He was very negative, very cutting." In 1988 several articles suggested that William E. Simon, an investment banker and former secretary of the Treasury, might buy Avis. (He did not.) According to Vittoria, the analyst responded by saying, "Bill Simon wouldn't be that stupid." Said Vittoria, "We attempted to indicate that this person didn't know what he was talking about, but we'd get frustrated. Well, we sat down and decided that anything we'd do [to strike back] would hurt. We felt that it would lead to more publicity. The greater the publicity you generate, the more the story hangs around."

Frustrating as it may be, accepting the occasional negative article is just a cost of doing business. "These are big, influential companies, trying to use us to sell products," said Paul Carroll of *The Wall Street Journal.* "They need to be prepared to take their lumps."

A story in print is already in print. You cannot undo what everybody has already seen. Pulling advertising or cutting off communication is emotionally satisfying but ineffective in blunting the damage of a story that's appeared, and it's unlikely to improve future coverage, especially by national publications or networks. Beyond writing a letter detailing your disagreement with the piece, there is little to be done . . . now. The effective CEO, however, immediately starts positioning himself for the next time. "Let one or two months go by," said Shepard of *Business Week.* "Then call and say, 'I'd like to come in and have lunch with the editors and reporters covering the beat. We just want to tell you what our position is.' That's the smart way to handle it."

"The worst thing you can do is not talk to them after you've been blasted," said Pete Silas. Peter Dowd heads right for the source. "We go to the reporter and jawbone, to reinforce our perspective, so that next time they can get it right," said Dowd. "Also, it's very important to get them to update their computer files, because otherwise other reporters will pick up the same facts when they sit down to do the next stories. You don't want the same story to keep haunting you."

What's most important in times of leaks and bad news is to recall your agenda. The incidents that flare up seem all-consuming at the time, but focusing on a single stinging article or even one fiasco is the short-term approach. People forget fast. Today's scandal is tomorrow's trivia question. A media strategy is not about short-term damage control; it's about putting your story across over the long haul.

THE CITIZENS OF ONLY ONE CONTINENT ON EARTH HAVE YET TO RELY ON THE CITATION V.

Across six continents and 38 countries, the Citation V is the fastest-selling business jet in history. It outsells all other competing aircraft – jet or turboprop – because it outperforms them in so many ways. Yet its operating costs are guaranteed to be lower than any competing airplane.

Year after year, on financial statements throughout the world, the Citation V is one bird that looks very good in black and white.

THE SENSIBLE CITATIONS

Cessna
A Textron Company

Chapter Nine

THE ROLE OF PUBLIC RELATIONS

Public-relations staffers are the Rodney Dangerfields of the corporate world. They can't get any respect. "The PR people want to be your friends," said one business reporter. "They want to take you out to lunch. Everybody knows they're there to tell you a bunch of bull."

Flacks inundate reporters with reams of ridiculous releases, barrage them with phone calls promoting some new sprocket. Just as annoying are the PR departments that stand in the way of information-gathering. "Many press people are just there to obfuscate, to stall, to block access," said Laura Landro of *The Wall Street Journal*.

The sad truth is that executives often share the reporters' disdain. "PR is the most disliked department in the company," said a senior officer at an East Coast utility company. "The staffers are slime bags, always putting on a happy face and not telling the truth."

Perhaps that's because in many companies public relations has the wrong role. The PR staff is rarely included in the inner circle of management. In many companies this department in charge of disseminating information doesn't know what's going on. "PR people do not necessarily occupy the highest level in companies," said PR executive Gershon Kekst. "They are frequently the last to know." Because they are brought into the loop only after problems arise, they are forever playing catch-up. As if this powerlessness weren't hard enough, PR departments are frequently required to shoulder the blame when an unflattering piece appears in the press. "Many CEOs hold PR responsible for the output of the press, the same way the factory manager is responsible for the output of the factory," said Stephen Shepard of *Business Week*. "They're told, 'If the story is negative, it's your fault.' Well, that's an unreasonable burden."

Years ago at Westinghouse Electric, a CEO fuming about a negative article in a national publication summoned his corporate spokesperson. "Have that reporter fired!" said the CEO. "What?" said the spokesperson. "I'm serious," the CEO said. "We're a big company. We advertise a lot. Get that guy fired!"

There are many things PR people can't do. But what *should* they be doing? At a company like American Airlines, 4,000 to 5,000 calls come in weekly from reporters requesting information and interviews. The job of the public-relations staffers is to assess these requests, funnel them to the right people, and channel information that flows to the outside. "They're the traffic cops," said William Alley of American Brands. "They're the expediters. They run the railroad."

The PR staffers are also the bridge builders as you construct a long-term relationship with the press. Every time they come through for reporters—every time they return phone calls promptly with accurate information or set up an interview or suggest a well-formulated story idea—they build another bridge. No journalist expects to talk to the CEO every time he calls. And journalists understand that the PR person will be speaking from the company's point of view. But reporters don't want stalling or equivocation or lies.

In some progressive companies, the PR group has also begun to play a new role: helping formulate the media plan and the messages—under CEO supervision. In this way the communications group becomes a central player, not an adjunct. "It's a big shift from when I was hired 13 years ago," said Grant Horne of PG&E. "Back then policy was established by management, and then the PR head was called in to tell people about it. Now PR participates in the discussion. PR sits at the management table."

In progressive companies like these, there is a greater awareness that the actions and decisions of any corporation—public or private—have public ramifications. The PR representative at the management table keeps the company's eyes focused on what these ramifications may be and how the press and public are likely to react to corporate behavior.

"There's little you can do in a company this size that doesn't have some PR spinoff," said Peter Dowd of Texaco. "Anything—new equipment, new products—has some impact on one or more of your constituencies. You've got to be able to communicate. That's just as important as bricks and mortar. You have to sell your point of view. That's the political side of running a business."

This new-style PR department is the creator and keeper of the media plan, the guardian of core messages. That should be its main occupation. Here's how Kekst put it: "The job of PR is to say, 'Your business strategy is this, right? You're going to measure yourself this way, right? Okay, the public dimension is this. And to succeed you're going to need these people to be supportive. Here's how you're going to reach these people. And along the way, here are the possible traps. You're building a new plant, for example. There may be environmental problems, consumer problems—these are the risks, the crises. And this is the way to win consistent support.'" A PR professional must say, in essence, "Here is our communications strategy. I have analyzed the company's goals. This is our audience; this is our set of messages. Let's get to work."

Giving the department that role is a valuable way to use PR. Few companies do it. Perhaps few PR staffs are up to the task, or perhaps management doesn't want to empower this lower-level group. It certainly requires a different way of thinking. But in this capacity PR is making a much more significant contribution to the corporate effort. At forward-thinking firms such as Corning, General Electric, and American Brands, as well as PG&E, the top communications executive sits in on core management deliberations and consults on the media dimensions of decisions before rather than after the fact.

Yet no matter how you use your communications department, several troublesome questions remain for you as CEO: How can you tell if your PR department is effective? What measurements can you use? Just totaling the number of positive and negative news pieces is misleading. If your PR was better, if your media plan was better, would you be getting better press? Or are the PR staffers doing a Herculean task just to help you get the press you have? Different industries use different benchmarks, but the main tool is the survey—public-opinion and employee polls. NCR, the AT&T-owned computer and systems manufacturer in Dayton, Ohio, gauges the effectiveness of its PR staff by hiring an outside firm to poll reporters.

Since the late '80s consulting firms have sprung up to assess the effectiveness of media strategies. You send them your key messages and your target media, and they look at how often your themes are picked up within a specified time period. Unfortunately most of these groups are better at spewing out numbers and bar charts illustrating how often certain phrases or themes appear in print or on the air than in the subtler analysis of your message's effectiveness.

In the end the CEO has to take on this subjective task himself. Luckily he needs to ask only one question: Have our contacts with the press helped or hindered this company in reaching its objectives? Everything else is secondary.

IF THERE WERE A CITATION FAMILY REUNION, THE GROUP PHOTO WOULD LOOK LIKE THIS.

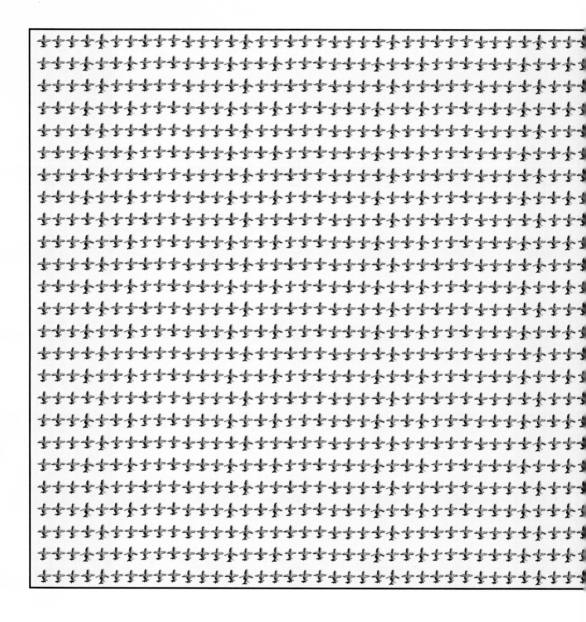

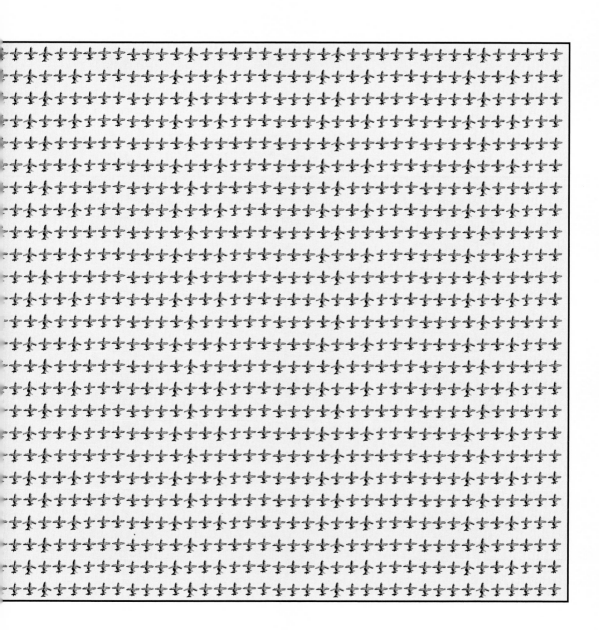

When the first Citation was delivered in 1972, its competitors had a big head start. They'd been selling in the same market for nearly a decade.

But buyers know a superior product when they see one. And they began buying Citations. Today, the worldwide Citation fleet has grown to 2,000 and counting. The Citation family has expanded to six models.

And something else keeps growing larger and larger, too. Citation's lead over those competitors who had that big head start.

THE SENSIBLE CITATIONS

Cessna
A Textron Company

Chapter Ten

THE ROLE OF THE CEO

 media strategy will never work unless the CEO takes the time to make it work. For him to close the door on pressing day-to-day commitments and ponder a vision and story for his company is no simple task. Yet a media strategy born of a clear vision needs to be on the executive's checklist as surely as satisfying customers and increasing shareholder value. What, after all, could be more central than defining the company for the staff and for the world outside?

If the CEO weaves the narrative—where the company is, where it's going—does that mean he alone should deliver it? What is the CEO's role in a media strategy? What kind of personal image should he cultivate?

The public persona of the CEO has gone through several transformations over the last 40 years. In the 1950s and '60s he was the man in the gray flannel suit: a boring businessman—better paid than many, but not much better known. By the 1980s, as business and finance became news, the man in gray flannel became a Master of the Universe. Some speculate that the press, in its thirst for personalities—having exhausted movie, TV, sports, and fashion celebrities—was creating a new class of celeb-

During his tenure as chairman and CEO of Chrysler, Lee Iacocca (left) epitomized the superstar executive, even appearing on the hit TV show Miami Vice *with actor Edward James Olmos.*

◆

rity: the superstar CEO. Of course, it didn't hurt that in the deregulated and highly leveraged 1980s business was the great game—flashy and daring. CEOs were profiled in glitzy mass-market publications like *Manhattan, Inc.*—a genre journalists called "the executive as rock star." In the new corporate cult of personality, Chrysler chairman Lee Iacocca and Time Warner co-chairman Steven J. Ross were turning up on the covers of not only *Fortune* and *Forbes* but *Time, Newsweek,* and *People.*

Beyond the glory-hogging of certain flashy executives, however, some CEOs have sought fame for legitimate business reasons: in a marketing-driven age, the better known the CEO, the more consumers can identify his face, and the more they may pick out and buy his company's products. R. David "Dave" Thomas, founder and CEO of Wendy's International, and Frank Perdue, founder of Perdue Farms, a poultry company in Salisbury, Maryland, continue this CEO-as-spokesman strategy, establishing themselves as living logos for their products. The more popular they become, the more popular their product—or so goes the theory.

By the early '90s, however, when words like *recession*, *budget deficit*, and *unemployment* began turning up regularly on the nightly news, sensitive executives knew that the glitz act was wearing thin. Stories about CEOs and their speedboats or swanky beach houses seemed poorly timed. Now Steve Ross was back on covers being attacked for his extravagant compensation. Superstar financiers Donald Trump and John H. Gutfreund became the punch lines of jokes about excess. For many CEOs, the '90s hit like the hangover after the party '80s.

Today a new paradigm is evolving. Fewer executives want to be known as million-dollar superstars. The new goal is to keep the emphasis on the company, not the man. James Smith, chairman of First American, speaks for many when he derides egotism in CEOs. "Business people have got to be extremely careful about trying to get too much publicity," he said. "Iacocca did more damage than good to Chrysler through PR. Here was [former CEO John] Akers always in the newspaper, and IBM had more problems than ever. And look at John Reed at Citicorp. The more publicity the CEO gets, the worse shape the company is in." Celebrity-CEO posturing is clearly out of vogue. The Smith credo for the '90s is this: The more you expose yourself, the more you become a target. Or as they say in Japan, the nail that sticks up gets pounded down.

Alan M. Webber, co-founder of *Fast Company*, a business and management magazine, and a past editorial director of the *Harvard Business Review*, described "the rise of the egoless corporation" in a 1991 article for *The Wall Street Journal*. In examining the faceless Japanese business model, he asked top Japanese executives, "Why is it, with so much U.S. market share in so many consumer product industries, almost no Japanese CEOs are known to American consumers? Wouldn't it make sense for Japanese companies to introduce their CEOs to Americans, to let us see the people whose products we are buying, to humanize the products, to give us a feeling for the character of the company? The resounding answer was no. At Toyota, Toshiba, Matsushita, Ricoh, and elsewhere, what the Japanese executives told me was this: 'We are selling our products, not our CEOs, to consumers. We want our products to speak for themselves. If our CEO were to change, retire, or step down, we wouldn't want our customers' view of the products to change. And besides, the CEO is not that important in the scheme of the whole organization.'"

In the '90s most American CEOs have gotten back to basics. They're dedicated to keeping their companies lean and efficient. They've put the focus back on the business rather than on themselves. And yet communication remains a necessity. What role does that dictate for the chief executive? Even if the CEO is not a star, he is still the main spokesman. He must step forward to deliver fundamental, urgent messages. No one else can speak with the same authority.

But a new trend is evolving, a corporate philosophy that puts the emphasis on the company, not the CEO. A few chief executives, like Pete Silas of Phillips Petroleum and John Hall of Ashland Oil, have begun spreading the communications duties down through the company, sharing the spotlight. The policy grows naturally out of the current business climate favoring "empowerment." Executives are saying that the story is crucial, not the storyteller. As CEOs they have shaped their companies' messages. Who delivers them is less important.

For some corporate leaders, such a freewheeling attitude might seem inappropriate. Perhaps they think their position will be diminished as others assume communications duties once held only by the CEO. Perhaps they want to hang on to the spotlight for ego reasons. Or maybe they think any other system will lead to chaos. "What is this? Anarchy?," they might ask. "Is everyone out there talking for the company?"

To a greater or lesser extent, the answer is yes. Clearly no one but the CEO should speak on sensitive issues involving the stock, trade secrets, or earnings forecasts. Nor should anybody comment on areas outside his expertise. But employees have a stake in the company too. If they screw up and the company is hurt, they're affected—perhaps laid off. The staff will make mistakes from time to time, but according to CEOs who've tried sharing communications duties, the benefits far outweigh such mistakes.

"I encourage other people in the company to talk," said Silas. "The person closest to the situation should be able to comment. Yes, you take chances on their performing under pressure. But I'm willing to take that risk. You're not going to develop your people if you do it all yourself. And so far our experience has been good. It's surprising how people prove they can handle the responsibility. And we've improved our image by allowing it."

Hall, Silas, and the rest of this group of CEOs have let others talk for clear-cut business reasons. The CEO has too many responsibilities to always be the one talking to the press. The more others can step up, the better off the company image. When lower-level executives are brought into analysts' meetings, for example, the financial world sees that the company doesn't have just one strong leader, it also has a sharp team. "It's good for any company to let analysts and the press know there is depth of management," said John Hall.

The more your executives are exposed to the local press as they advance in the company, the more they're prepared to handle major media coverage when the time comes. You can send your junior executives to media-training classes—in fact, you probably should—but nothing takes the place of those first encounters with the local TV cameras or the first time they get misquoted, when a few of the words are right but the whole idea is wrong.

These are crucial experiences for executives as they are groomed for top management. Yet all too many staffers pay little attention to developing media skills. "What they really ought to do," said James Smith, "is spend years talking to newspapers and, over a period of time, gain experience." Joseph Vittoria of Avis echoed the sentiment: "I learned the ropes talking to trades, *Travel Agent, Business Travel News*, and to the local papers when I was the manager of Avis Europe."

There's also an odd side benefit to pushing your junior staffers and even factory employees forward—what I term the rule of inverse believability. For many journalists truth appears inversely proportional to rank. That is, the further down the company ladder the person you talk to, the more believable he seems. Reporters tend to believe a factory worker over a CEO 99 times out of 100. The assembly-line worker seems to have no ulterior agenda; the CEO has dozens. So the further down the CEO pushes the communications responsibility, the more honest and enlightened he and his company appear. "It's refreshing when the media has access to the people who actually do the work," said Jerre L. Stead, president of NCR.

In the June '92 issue of *Across the Board* magazine, Wayne Welch, founding editor of *Corporate Finance* magazine, argued that delegation of exposure is a logical outgrowth of the empowerment trend. "If people at lower and lower levels are encouraged to take on responsibility and to make decisions," said Welch, "then managements will most likely be forced to let them talk about it in public."

Beyond being "forced," the company may actually want lower-level employees to step forward and speak. The benefits here mirror those of any other type of empowerment. With greater trust, the staffers feel more responsible and involved. Because they've been allowed to speak for the team, they have a greater feeling of team spirit. In short, they're more fired up about their company. When you speak for an organization, you can't help but identify with it.

The staffers at Avis got this feeling when Vittoria allowed a *Fortune* reporter to fly around the country without any PR escort and talk to employees from coast to coast. "That was a real risk," said Vittoria. "Who knows what could have turned up?" What did turn up was a positive article and a proud staff. Pride is also what Pete Silas engenders when he sends security analysts to talk with Phillips executives for two days before they even see him.

How do you retain control? Not by clamping down or creating Big Brother paranoia. You retain control by delineating the direction of the company, by shaping the shared story of the business—a company myth that everyone is proud to be part of. Take the example of Silas, who encouraged analysts to talk to his staffers: "What makes me happy," he said, "is when they tell me that all of us in the company seem to be on the same page."

In his former position as CEO of Square D, an Illinois-based electrical equipment manufacturer, Jerre Stead became known as a champion of communications delegation. He encouraged everyone in the company to speak out; in fact, he made a policy of it.

At the start of his tenure in 1987, Stead and his top staff developed a vision complete with messages, principles, and plans. By early 1988 he had established "vision colleges," which each of his 23,000 employees attended. "Here is our mission, our strategic objectives, our financial target," he told employees. "They stay the same whether you're talking to newspapers, TV, or investment consultants."

What Stead was doing was enrolling every one of his employees as "associates" in the company story, preparing them to discuss the workings of Square D with the press. He urged the PR department to seek coverage for any employee who was making an impact on the corporation or the community—to create "local heroes." Employees were free to converse with the media as long as they stayed clear of topics that could affect the company's stock price. Stead said he was "happy to have anyone speak out. The more of those broad issues being addressed by the associates in the press, the better."

Stead's philosophy may seem extreme, but he is only acknowledging the obvious: employees can be valuable media assets. "The only sustainable advantage for a company over time is its people," said Stead. "They have to be an active part of where the company is going."

The CEO who can chart the direction—who can issue the major statements but then allow others to share in the excitement and the occasionally scary responsibility of conversing with the media—this CEO may be steering the smartest course for his company.

WHEN WE BUILD MODEL AIRPLANES AT CESSNA, NOBODY GETS GLUE ON THEIR FINGERS.

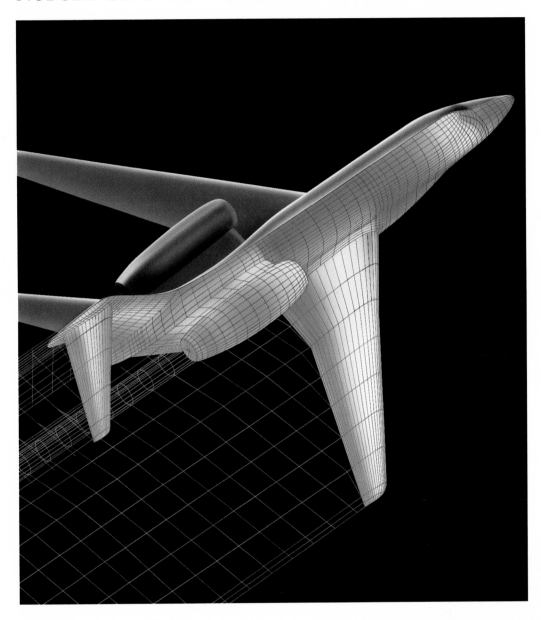

You're looking at a highly advanced computer model of the Citation X. The technology is called Computational Fluid Dynamics (CFD). And it was used to identify areas where airflow would reach transonic and supersonic speeds – allowing engineers to modify the shape of those areas to minimize aerodynamic drag. Before the Citation X, CFD had never been used to measure transonic air speeds on a business jet.

But before the Mach .9 Citation X, it had never really been necessary.

THE SENSIBLE CITATIONS

Cessna
A Textron Company

Chapter Eleven

The Anatomy of a Winning Strategy

T he story of Hewlett-Packard is a story of a major media turnaround, and it sums up many of the themes discussed so far. For years the company, based in Palo Alto, California, was perceived as a fusty old engineering instrumentation firm—a bunch of nerdy guys in glasses wandering around with slide rules and plastic pocket protectors. It turned out boring products like oscilloscopes and idiosyncratic pocket calculators that used "reverse Polish notation." When top executives, almost all of them engineers, sat down with the press, they talked about megabytes and gigabytes. Small wonder that even though the company was generating hundreds of millions of dollars, reporters' eyes glazed over at the mention of Hewlett-Packard. This media problem was all the more egregious because the company was one of the elite profiled by Tom Peters and Robert Waterman Jr. in their 1982 book *In Search of Excellence*. While HP's business fundamentals were strong, its media relations were less than excellent.

The problem peaked in 1983, when HP got into the flashy personal computer business, and still the press paid scant attention. Stories about its sexy young competitors, such as Sun Microsystems and Apple, regularly made the front pages. Although HP was one of the progenitors of Silicon Valley, it had been around so long and in such a dull way that it would have had a hard time buying coverage. "Nobody was writing about them," recalled one industry reporter. "They weren't getting all that 'glam' coverage of Silicon Valley. They didn't have a cuddly whiz kid entrepreneur or any personality. They flew right under the press's radar." HP's inability to generate excitement among business reporters and potential customers was hurting sales. Management knew something had to change but wasn't sure where to start.

A decade later Hewlett-Packard is one of America's most sophisticated companies in its approach to the press. HP has a five-year media plan that includes a set of objectives, strategies, and major messages. It has forged a powerful partnership with the media, transforming its image from fuddy-duddy to savvy and high-tech. It has garnered strong, frequent coverage highlighting the themes it believes are important. And the business isn't doing badly either—annual sales were up by almost $2 billion in 1992.

What changed? The company's attitude, said Roy E. Verley, director of corporate communications. "We've come a long way from the old days when the media was the enemy. We went through an education process. Today we see the media as a vital component of our success. Not many companies have that attitude. A lot say they do, but they still regard the media as extensions of their marketing departments. They only want to work with them when they can hype a product. They write thank you letters when a favorable article appears. All that reflects a remarkable naiveté. You'll never succeed if you think the press is in business to flatter you."

CEO John A. Young, now retired, and Verley set out to build a relationship with the press. They instituted an "adopt-an-editor" program in which senior managers formed relationships with the editors of local papers or trade journals. At least once every quarter they would ask the editors to lunch. Top management would sometimes meet with the editorial boards of major publications as well. Day by day the PR department would attempt to return press calls within 15 minutes and certainly before deadlines. And everyone in the company was trying to speak

1990

Former chief executive John Young (left) and Roy Verley, Hewlett-Packard's director of corporate communications, developed a media plan that transformed HP's image from that of a plodding bureaucracy of computer nerds into that of a hip, high-tech industry leader.

◆

a new language to the media: English. The techno-speak of the engineering executives was banished. "Effective communications is our responsibility," said Verley. "It's not the role of the press to have to interpret our lingo."

Hewlett-Packard also set out to get more sophisticated about the way the press works, to try to understand it publication by publication, writer by writer—what their interests are, who their readers are. For every interview, Young would receive a briefing memo, not just about the reporter's topic, but also his background: This reporter has been with the publication so long and covers this beat; he has a detailed knowledge of this subject matter; this is his audience.

As HP's approach to interviews evolved, Roy Verley had a realization: "We were always good on response. But we didn't seem to have a plan. We were more spontaneous, intuitive. There was nothing organized—no agreed-upon messages that said, 'This is what HP is all about.'"

Verley talked with Young, and the CEO's response was telling. "If you think we have all the messages tucked away," Young said, "and we just haven't shared them with you, you're wrong. Why don't you go out, develop a critical set of messages, then come back and present them to the management staff."

Said Verley: "I don't think our CEO woke up thinking of communication in a broad context. Most companies don't. Much of our industry is so busy inventing, creating, they don't think about long-term impact—'What does this all add up to?'"

Over the next month, Verley and his team, in consultation with Young and the company's executive committee, developed a set of major messages. Working on 10 issues, including financial performance, globalization, business fundamentals, outside alliances, and customer satisfaction, they took each issue and broke it into five categories:

• Issue Statement: Why is this topic important?

• Desired Perception: What impression do we want to create?

• Major Message: What do we want to say?

• Sub-Message: What's the meat of the argument, the evidence and examples?

• Barrier: What are the problems and weaknesses that contradict the message?

One example: Under the issue "People and Culture," the desired message to the employees was "HP is a good place to work." This was a key internal message. HP, slow for much of the '80s to respond to new market demand and hobbled by bureaucracy, watched its profitability fall almost every quarter in 1989 and '90, sometimes by 15 percent; the stock price fell from $75 to $25 a share. Between 1989 and 1992 the company laid off 6,000 employees, and many others shifted positions or retired early. So HP wanted to say, Our core values remain; we care about our people. The sub-message included a list of benefits such as health care and vacation time. The barrier: individual benefits at HP were not as lavish as those of some younger competitors. HP felt certain, however, that its benefits were among the industry's best.

Hewlett-Packard produced a 75-page document, a communications bible distributed to every staffer from general manager up. To this day every time an executive speaks before employees, outside groups, or reporters, he has the articulation of the company vision, the company blueprint, at his fingertips.

The next step was molding the messages into a media plan that would focus on the number-one corporate goal: improving profitability. What press actions would further that goal? The public saw HP as an engineering company making oscilloscopes for engineers. In fact, more than 70 percent of its revenues were coming from computers, but the public didn't realize it. HP had a fuzzy image. So the media goal was to transform the company's image into one of an aggressive long-term player in the computer business. The key audience was the chief financial officers who sign the purchase requisitions for their companies' computer systems.

John Young and his team set to work talking to the business press. Never before had they discussed divisional revenue figures publicly. Now, to demonstrate the strength of HP's computer business, they revealed what percentage of total sales came from computers. Every time an article appeared identifying HP as "the Palo Alto test equipment giant," someone would call the reporter and say, "We're in the computer business."

Of course, HP ran headlong into the communications strategy of its primary competitor, IBM. The strategy: what insiders called FUD—*fear*, *uncertainty*, and *doubt*. As the computer-industry leader, IBM was stirring up lots of uncertainty about its competitors, presumably hoping that buyers would conclude, "This computer stuff is so confusing, I guess I'll just go with the one I've heard of—IBM." FUD is always a strong strategy for the established player in a crowded field. Just ask Verley. "We felt FUDed out. We had better specs, a better service record. But the high-end customers didn't perceive us as a computer company." The media team developed a series of video pieces, magazine articles, and speeches—anything to position HP as a safe buy, a real computer company.

The startling differences in the before-and-after pictures of Hewlett-Packard highlight the effectiveness of a well-thought-out media strategy. In 1985 the stock price was tumbling. Earnings were falling 10 percent from the previous year, down to $489 million. The business media were asking, How long can HP hang on? How long will their customers stay loyal?

By contrast, in the first half of 1992, earnings were up 44 percent over the previous year, rocketing to $632 million for that six-month period alone. And the media? *The New York Times* ran a glowing article: HEWLETT-PACKARD NET TOPS WALL STREET EXPECTATIONS. *The Wall Street Journal* declared, HEWLETT-PACKARD IS TOO BUSY TO NOTICE INDUSTRY SLUMP and continued, "Not bad for a company once considered a torpid dinosaur among fleet-footed competitors." The *Business Week* headline said it all: SUDDENLY, HEWLETT-PACKARD IS DOING EVERYTHING RIGHT. Of course, the communications strategy was only partly responsible; HP also introduced its successful printers in these years. But good press and good sales often go hand in hand.

"We never had a sense of who we were, what we were trying to accomplish," said Roy Verley. "Finally we said, 'Let's take the randomness out of communication. What are we trying to say? What are our business goals? What are the key messages that grow out of that? Let's develop a systematic approach for delivering them.'"

The rest is history. Or at least the rough draft of history—journalism.

EPILOGUE

"ommunication is 80 percent of the game in management and leadership," according to Jerre Stead of NCR.

The chief executive is uniquely positioned to communicate. His high office is a ready-made platform, and when the CEO talks, his employees and constituencies will listen. And so will the media.

This visibility is a powerful tool, but what will the CEO do with it? How will he use it to capture the imagination of his company and the world beyond? There must be a guiding intelligence behind the communication, and most important, there must be a reason to communicate. That's the whole point of a media plan. Such a plan will not perform magic. It won't transform an ugly duckling into a swan. It won't singlehandedly save a corporation. What it can do is provide the right showcase for the company's strengths and the right vehicle for its messages.

In the end, whether a CEO chooses to take center stage or not, he is still the storyteller. He is the one who must weave the company narrative. The better the story he tells, the more he will inspire all of his constituencies, internal and external. And the more effectively that vision is communicated, the greater the chance it has of becoming reality.

IN SELECTING THE WORLD CHAMPION MIDSIZE JET, THE JUDGES HAVE REACHED A SPLIT DECISION.

Many owners say the Citation VI is the perfect midsize business jet. No other aircraft offers more speed and more stand-up cabin space for less money. Many other owners say the Citation VII is the world's best midsize jet. It's just as spacious as the VI, but it's even more powerful, more versatile, and more technically advanced.

So, is the ideal midsize jet the Citation VI or the Citation VII? Judging by the popularity of the two, we'd say the answer is "yes."

THE SENSIBLE CITATIONS

Cessna
A Textron Company